BARBARIAN SCIENCE

TOWN SQUARE BOOKS, INC.

BARBARIAN SCIENCE
JIM MCMURTRAY

Library of Congress Number: 99-75885
ISBN: 1-886017-22-0

Published by
Town Square Books, Inc.
Patricia Minter Grierson, Ph. D., Publisher
PO Box 55808
Jackson, MS 39296

Bar • bar • i • an - **1.** *n.* a savage, uncivilized person ‖ (for the ancient Greeks) a non-Greek ‖ (for the ancient Romans) a person from outside the Roman empire **2.** *adj.* of or like a barbarian [F. *barbarien*]

(Webster's Encyclopedic Dictionary of the English Language Deluxe Edition)

Bar • bar • i • an - *(adj.)* **1.** of or relating to a land, culture, or people alien and usually believed to be inferior to one's own; **2.** lacking refinement, gentleness, learning, or artistic or literary culture; **3.** of or relating to a people or group in a stage of cultural development about midway between savagery and full civilization.

(Webster's Third International Dictionary Unabridged)

Bar • bar • i • an - **1.** *n.* a person perceived as wanting what you have and possessing the means to acquire it **2.** *adj.* of or relating to such disquieting persons.

(The author)

Foreword

A colleague of mine once said that no student should pass through a university without taking at least one course from a naturalist – someone who could walk with you along the beach, pick up a handful of sand, and talk with you for hours about what he or she sees there. Think how much was captured in that one wish. First was the desire for the student to be exposed to science in the raw – science stripped of most of its trappings and dealt with as an extension of human experience and an exploration of human curiosity. The definition of "naturalist" was itself chosen to suggest how science should be presented to young minds, drawing the listener into the fold and the discussion. The image of the walk along the beach was also intended to rule out science as mindless memorization of terms and blind acceptance of dogma or purported final answers. It was plainly not intended to rule out the teacher as sometime provider of information or leader of Socratic dialogue about scientific theory. After all, the student wouldn't see much in the sand at first, and something like natural selection would surely have come up along the way, wouldn't it? One can even imagine the conversation shifting from the sand to the stars, completely oblivious of disciplinary boundaries crossed en route.

In this wonderful little book, Jim McMurtray, astronomer, teacher and friend, conveys these and many other important ideas in a unique manner and style born of his own life's experience. A glance at the Table of Contents will tell you the enormous range of things touched upon: science literacy, science research, university science, school science, science teaching, and ancient science, plus a list of other topics that can best be described as "for all X, science and X". The variable X ranges from religion to art, economics, politics, engineering, the movies, and the press. Given the breadth and the brevity of the book, it could hardly be a philosophical treatise on any of the above. It wasn't intended to be. But it has quite insightful things to say in each of its commentaries. And that is not an easy thing to do. There are also a couple of "surprise" sections that we won't mention, because we don't want to spoil them for you.

If that is what the book is about, what is it like? That's easy to answer: In a nutshell, this book is like Jim McMurtray himself. It is irreverent, at times heretical. It is insightful, at times wise. It is laced with wit and humor throughout. It has many serious things to say, yet it never takes itself too seriously. It shines spotlights on unattired emperors, especially those whom others see as fully clothed.

Yes, you say, but what is its message? The principal topic is science literacy – both its importance and our continuing failures to come to grips with it, as we trip over our own formalisms and institutional structures. If you are interested in issues of science literacy, "general science" or "science and the public", then this book is must reading. So too should it be for those interested in education reform and revitalization. But it is not a book for specialists. It can and should be read by all those interested in what science is about. There is wisdom in McMurtray's words of science.

One final thing: We promise that you won't be neutral about this little book after you read it, especially if you are part of the science or science education establishments. But, even if you get angry almost as often as you laugh, it will make you think. And that is its purpose.

Kenneth M Hoffman
Professor of Mathematics Emeritus
Massachusetts Institute of Technology
Madison, Maryland   October 3, 1999

Introduction

*T*his is a book about science for the thoughtful barbarian. Barbarians of course, are those who are ignorant of the noble customs, practices and rituals of any given group of non-barbarians. You might prefer *not* to think of yourself as a barbarian, but we all find ourselves outside *somebody's* gate from time to time. If you feel that you are outside the gates of science, you have probably found yourself in the good company of many other barbarians and you may already have come to the conclusion that rightfully, science belongs to everybody. Science is for barbarians too.

Fascination with the universe and its various mechanisms is common to almost all members of our curious species. There is no privileged information in science and there are no restrictions on who may pursue it. If parts of it have been systematically walled off, then those walls were built in secret without anyone's permission, and they need to come down.

To some of those non-barbarians on the inside it may be very important that you do not acquire the "special knowledge" that they have. Barbarism, after all, is the baseline from which superiority is calculated. Without a minimum number of barbarians, they might be altogether unremarkable. The more one is "surrounded by barbarians," the more exalted one becomes.

This can lead to the establishment of an elaborate, regulated brokerage for dispensing the information. This serves to keep the number of barbarians up to acceptable levels. Unfortunately, any attempt at manipulating their numbers quickly produces a sizable horde.

Perhaps we can no longer afford to maintain a single path to science, screened and controlled to filter out the unworthy.

Science literacy is of vital importance to our society now. It can no longer be confined to a special inner circle. Perhaps we need to open the gates and let the so-called barbarians in. We should probably do this fairly soon because the horde is getting bigger and they are beginning to make frightening noises....

Table of Contents

Science Literacy

*T*he universe is mostly empty space. Scattered here and there in all that empty space, there are atoms. The empty space is all of the locations where the atoms aren't. According to the model we currently use, the atoms themselves are mostly empty space. *This* empty space consists of all the locations inside the atom where the elementary particles that make up the atom are, at any given moment, not. The universe then, is a very large number of potential places for things to be. Fortunately, we only have to deal with where they actually wound up.

Science is the rational and systematic study of how all of the various arrangements of empty space and tiny bits of stuff interact together over time. We study this from every conceivable perspective so that we can make some sort of sense of the universe. Scientific literacy consists of knowing a few general, basic things about that quest. Literacy does not mean you have to be current in every field or in any one of them. It means that you have some modest understanding of where we humans are right now in the long process of sorting things out.

The only rational response to the universe in which we find ourselves is baffled amazement. If you are really paying attention, then you will be constantly surprised, confused, and astonished. Where we are right now is probably not a special place. It is more likely that this is just another point along the line in the unfolding history of our species. If all of it makes perfect sense to you now, then you must be missing big chunks of it. It has taken us a while to get this far and we are far from finished. Those people who *have* achieved total comprehension of their world have done so at the price of confining themselves to a very small and attenuated cosmos with no windows.

I have been amazed, amused, heartened, dismayed, and perplexed by our ambivalent love affair with science. We human beings seem to have a natural passion for it. Whether we call ourselves professional scientists, serious amateurs or "science-free," we are fascinated with our world and we fiddle with it and puzzle over it constantly. Rarely do we find a person who is genuinely uninterested in the array of stimuli that we collectively call reality. When we do find one of these people, even casual conversation is difficult.

I stood once in the center of a large greenhouse full of all sorts of exotic and temperamental flora. I was listening to a tiny woman in her eighties as she explained to me that she had never had the slightest interest in science. She said she was at a loss to understand the fascination that so many people seemed to have with it. As she spoke to me, she was carefully examining the soil in a lush, thick pot of African violets. There were live green things growing off of every surface. "I'm just more partial to the *natural* things," she said. I doubt that she ever considered herself science literate, but she was curious about everything and there were few things that she could not discuss.

Most of us know a lot of science. The quality of this information varies considerably. Perhaps we know a lot of old science. Maybe we are obsessively current but narrowly focused. Some of us know a lot of stuff that is questionable, fanciful, whimsical, esoteric, exotic, or simply wrong. Some of these things we were taught, some we figured out all by ourselves and some of them we *just know*. Some of it is real and some of it is dogma. Literacy is not about knowing all the answers though; it's about understanding the questions.

Education alone, even in massive doses it seems, does not ensure science literacy. An advanced degree affords one not the slightest protection against being dead wrong. When we were in school we memorized a whole bunch of "answers." There is nothing wrong with that really, so long as the answers were *right*, they never change, and assuming we understood the question in the first place. The trouble is some of the answers *do* change and our

2

"common body of knowledge" does not always move along with the current.

My own science background is partly current science, partly science history and partly folk wisdom, myth, and misconception. I got every bit of it from "authoritative sources." I imagine yours is similarly composed. Unfortunately some of us have bought into the idea that a handful of special people know all the answers and if we can just acquire this information from them, then we will be literate. This hasn't worked before. Why should it work now?

You have learned a lot of stuff over the past few years. How reliable is this knowledge? How good are your sources? They were certainly authoritative, but were they infallible?

A number of years ago in a survey conducted at a prestigious Ivy League university which need not be named, it was revealed that a significant fraction of the graduates possessed less than total mastery of middle school Earth Science fundamentals.[1] Now I'm just guessing of course, but I suspect your alma mater wouldn't do any better. So what is the quality of *your* science education?

Does the Moon go around the Earth in a circle or in an ellipse? No, it doesn't. It actually follows a stretched out and snaky path that bears little resemblance to either shape. It most assuredly does go *around* the Earth, but never in a circle and never in an ellipse.

It is very likely that you were taught by some well-educated people that it *does* follow a near circular path. Almost certainly there were drawings in many of your science texts that showed the moon orbiting the Earth in a circle or an ellipse. This is science dogma. It is well-established, well-understood, widely accepted even by many notable professional scientists, and it is thoroughly, irreconcilably wrong.

Johannes Kepler might have explained it to you, but he died in 1630. We must assume that most of the science teachers and

---

[1] Harvard.

professors who came after him either never learned it, didn't consider it important enough to mention, or figured it was just way too complicated to teach. After all, it *looks* like it goes around in a circle so what's the difference?

Well, the Sun *looks* like it goes around the Earth too, but we don't teach *that* anymore do we? The fact is that neither a circular nor an elliptical path is possible. It simply won't work that way because the Earth has to move fairly fast in order to orbit about the Sun in 365 and a quarter days. The Moon though, orbits the Earth only about 12 times in that one-year span. The Moon's path might look like a sine wave except for the fact that the radius of the Earth's orbit is so large and it is moving so fast that the Moon's path is *never* convex to the Sun! That is, it never curves outward away from the Sun.

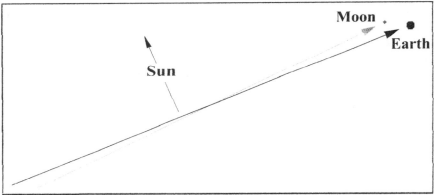

This schematic diagram (not to scale) shows a small portion of the Earth's orbital path around the Sun. It illustrates the Moon's actual path around the Earth. The Moon is dragged along as the Earth orbits so it swings inside, then outside the Earth's path as it completes each trip around us. From here of course, it appears to go around in a nearly circular path.

When we simplify something that is very complex, we run the risk of crossing that amorphous boundary between understandable and wrong. This has always been a dilemma in education. There are many similar examples.

Most people have observed that when the moon is close to the horizon it will frequently appear red or orange to the eye. We also may report that it seems larger at those times than when it is high overhead. This often generates questions from curious and observant children.

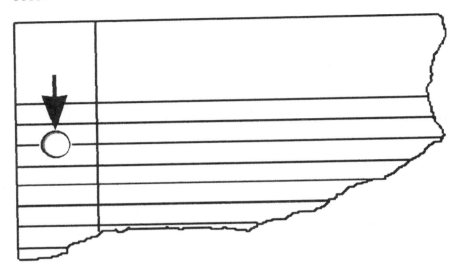

Does the apparent diameter of the Moon change when it is low on the horizon? Well, no actually it doesn't. That is an illusion (and a *good* one too because it sure looks like it does). You can measure it for yourself with a standard paper hole.

The full Moon will fit entirely inside one of the holes in a sheet of notebook paper when that paper is held at arm's length from your eye. I know you don't believe that, but it is true anyway. Try it. You will also see that it fits inside that hole at *any time*, regardless of how close the Moon is to the horizon.

I can remember teachers and other respected adults explaining to me that the Moon looks bigger when it is close to the horizon because the lower layers of the atmosphere distort and "magnify" the image. This simply does not happen. That huge orange Moon is a little trick that our brains play on us through visual association. When you actually measure it, there is no visually discernable difference in the Moon's apparent diameter.

If you can't trust the textbooks, you can't trust the experts and you can't even trust your own senses, how in blazes are you ever going to make yourself literate? Well, I guess you will just have to use some judgement and make some personal choices. That's what scientists have to do every day. That, in fact is the essence of literacy. Yeah, I know, that's harder than memorizing answers but that's just the way it is.

Atoms are human artifacts just like hours, minutes and seconds. We created the atomic model to explain why things behave the way they do.[1] It works beautifully. We have done such a good job of teaching the model that some students believe that sub-atomic particles are actually observed to possess the colors and shapes that we use to illustrate them in books or that you can see them with a special microscope.

We made up the atom to describe something we cannot experience directly with our senses.[2] The model describes something that is absolutely real, but the model itself is the brilliant work of many scientists working over many years. They deserve credit for this extraordinarily useful idea. It's not a discovery; it's a creation! Part of being literate in science is knowing the difference. It might also be useful to know the difference between a theory and an observation.

Evolution is *not* a theory. It is an observation. It is observable that species evolve. This is not in dispute. However they may have *originated*, they do evolve over time. Natural selection as the origin of species, on the other hand, *is* a theory. It is never too late to learn the difference between a theory and an observation.

Charles Darwin suggested that the evolutionary processes that we commonly observe in nature might account for the origin of existing species including Man. This, he said would come about through millions of years of natural selection. He didn't boldly declare that all species are continually evolving, because that was

---

[1] The concept of the atom was first introduced by the Greek philosopher, Democratus. He is perhaps better known for a series of great debates with arch philosophical rival, Republicus.

[2] Scientists create models to explain how things work. This is perfectly legal in all 50 states and throughout most of the world. Some people think scientists just "discover" things or find stuff that we didn't even know was lost.

(and is) common knowledge. He would have assumed everybody already knew that.

When someone says, "I don't believe in Evolution." What they probably *really* mean is: "I don't subscribe to Darwin's theory of the origin of Man." If that is what they mean, then *that* is what they should say. Saying that you don't believe in evolution is really a bit like saying you don't believe in gravity. You're free to say anything you like of course but I wouldn't want to go mountain climbing with you if you really feel that way.

A big part of being scientifically literate is just being literate. The language of science is necessarily precise. It is easy to get things wrong when we generalize. The words we use are important. Clouds are not made of water *vapor*. They are made of liquid water *droplets*. Water vapor is invisible. (I learned that as a child but I have had to learn it again several times.) The distinction seems to have some difficulty finding a comfortable place to curl up in my brain.

The point here is that we all carry with us our own peculiar collection of misconceptions and myths. One of the *biggest* myths is that *all* science professionals have broad general knowledge in *all* the sciences. Where on Earth did we ever get such an idea? Clearly this did not arise from observation. Where also did we get the idea that science is only for the few and the chosen?

A curious and well-read man or woman of modest academic background, *may be* more broadly literate in science than the chair of your Physics Department. I understand that this is a heresy, but it's quite accurate. The chairman of the Physics Department probably agrees with that statement in principle, but would have recommended the chairman of Biological Sciences as a better example.

Science is not the exclusive province of the formally trained and it never has been. We can tightly regulate the accreditation of science professionals, but we have no way of restraining the minds of renegade gardeners and shoe salesmen who just happen to be

7

intellectually gifted and curious. Formal science has not collected and nurtured all the bright intellects in our society. We have missed quite a few in fact and we are poorer for that.

We have, all of us, allowed an unfortunate and unnecessary gulf to open between professional science and the people it serves. It is not too late to start filling in that expanse. Perhaps this is the perfect time to begin. Information has never been more accessible, and professional science has never been more motivated to enlarge its circle of friends.

Distressing though it may be, it appears that we will enter the new millennium with superstition, myth, and pseudo-science still alive and flourishing. While we open new windows into nature and draw closer to understanding our environment, some of our citizens still walk on the dark side. Somehow we have disenfranchised a segment of our population. Somehow we have failed to share with them the human birthright of science. It is time for us to start repairing this damage we have done to ourselves.

A scientifically literate populace is essential to our continued development and perhaps to our survival. We cannot achieve this if we continue to teach that science is reserved for trained professionals and only to be approached by a chosen few, recognized and ordained to engage in the pursuit.

There is not much difference at all between "ordinary" people and those science professionals in the "Secret Inner Circle." They do not know everything, and *you* are not an innocent. You can talk to them and discover this for yourself or you can continue to believe that they are an evolutionary step or two above you. They won't mind that of course. Being perceived as an exalted wizard of science and a master of the mysterious forces of the universe is heady wine indeed.

Actually our history is filled with stories of "ordinary" people who excelled in science. The Wright brothers are one example. Wilber and Orville flew off the ground in 1903 in a craft they built together in blissful ignorance of the fact that such contraptions can't fly.[1] Milton Hummason didn't understand that muleskinners cannot comprehend astrophysics and Albert Einstein never figured out that science and mathematics are only for good students. We learn from history of course but apparently it takes very large amounts of it to produce any impact.

Who was it that determined the "proper" scope and sequence with which we all are exposed to scientific ideas? How did that person manage to discover the one right way, the one correct linear sequence for everyone to learn science? What great genius established this sacred and unalterable order of carefully metered doses of science that is still used today to process all students through the system? History does not tell us.[2]

To fully understand your role in the universe you need to know exactly where you are. You know that you live on a planet in orbit about a yellow dwarf star. We used to believe it was the other way around, but we got better.

Everything we know of that has ever lived on the Earth has lived in that thin film of intermingling fluids between the bottom of the ocean and the upper reaches of the atmosphere. That "biosphere" is the tiny percentage of the Earth's volume that supports life. On a standard globe you could represent the biosphere of the Earth with a few layers of plastic wrap. It is like the membrane of a soap bubble.

But that is not *where* you live. The Earth is not a location. It's just the thing you live on; or rather it's the thing that the biosphere you live *in* adheres *to*. The Earth is not a location because it is moving. It moves a lot actually. The space it is moving through is the space around that yellow dwarf star. It travels at about eighteen miles per second, so you are in a different place now than when you were at the top of the paragraph. You've moved. That

---

[1]   In 1902, a year and a half before the Wright's first flight at Kitty Hawk, Simon Newcomb, the renowned and highly respected American scientist, mathematician, and economist issued the following statement: "Flight by machines heavier than air is unpractical and insignificant, if not utterly impossible." Newcomb was awarded the Nobel Prize for Hubris in 1917.

[2]   Maybe it was Simon Newcomb.

is, *we've* moved. The whole thing has moved. And you'll never be back to where you were because the whole system is moving and the system it's part of is moving and the system *that* system is part of is moving too.

So the truth is, that you have *no idea* where you are, and neither does the President, the Congress, the United Nations nor all of the worlds great scientists.. Now, remember that, because it will help you to appreciate the various roles we all play in the grand scheme of things. It also gives us a very good benchmark for assessing our knowledge of ourselves.

The Biosphere

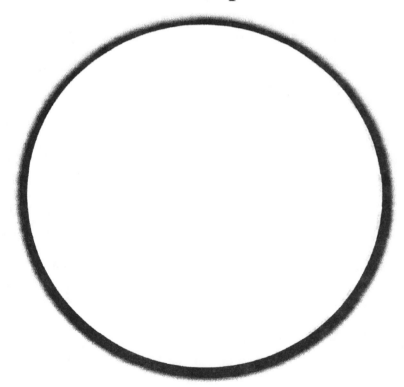

Earth's biosphere indicated in black. (Not to scale.)

University Science

*U*niversities teach science as a body of knowledge. Mostly they teach the *history* of science. There is nothing wrong with this at all. What else can we do really? There is much to understand about the history and culture of science that is vital to understanding its current state. There are principles and fundamentals with which we must be familiar if we are to pursue a career in the sciences. It is necessary sometimes to freeze parts of the corpus of science in order to teach it; otherwise it may be too fluid to capture in a three-hour course.

We are aware that it is constantly changing, but we must arrest it somewhere in order to transmit it to students. We try to warn them not to accept it as holy writ and not to allow it to become dogma, but sometimes we fail to get their attention or they do not listen. We should remind students constantly that by the standards of next century, our present perceptions may be considered "quaint." They might even be considered hysterically funny.

You have to take a slice of it somewhere then, because the answers can change *during* the final exam. Where one takes this "core sample" is of some importance. It should not be so far removed from current scientific work that it is outmoded before it can be used. Also it should not be incoherent because of active turbulence. History is fascinating business, but it doesn't make a hell of a lot of sense while you are making it

Right now we are puzzling over the size and age of the universe. We're *pretty* sure that is somewhere around half as big or twice as large as we think it *might* be... and probably about that old too. It would be unwise to select a single current view and teach that as fact when there is so much more that must be known

11

before the verdict can be rendered. What we teach in science (or should teach) is current working models, not dogma.

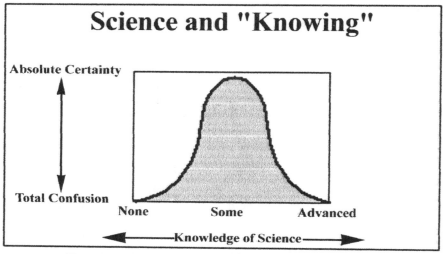

Science and "Knowing"

Degree of Certainty and Knowledge of Science

Persons with <u>no</u> knowledge of science are totally confused. Those with <u>advanced</u> knowledge of science are also totally confused. People with <u>some</u> knowledge of science know everything. Most of the people in the latter group have college degrees.

A scientific theory is a reasoned explanation of why things behave the way they do. There may be many competing models. If the universe reveals some different and unanticipated behavior tomorrow, then current models will have to be modified or replaced. That's a rule and everybody plays by it. It really does not matter at all how much you loved the older model or how "perfect" it seemed or how philosophically satisfying it may have been. You can't hold it as viable if it is lying still and cold at the bottom of a sudden avalanche of new information. We do a disservice to students when we do not teach them to expect this to happen on a regular basis.

How many times have you heard a professor say, "There is a reasonable chance that much of what you will learn in this course is wrong and will be replaced before your children reach high school."? Now you just might want to hold on to the notes from that class. There is a reasonable chance that professor may have made *other* intelligent statements.

The best advice a science student can receive is to beware of the "truth" and avoid association with those who have it. Sure, it might actually be right, but truth is an awfully big word so it is used sparingly in science and with much caution. Science is *not* a body of knowledge. It is a work in progress.

Even the best science education has a very short shelf life. You can't *master* it really; you can only pursue it. It is a lifelong endeavor and if you do it well, it is never finished.

Most universities do research in addition to teaching the lore of science. This is a good thing. It quickens the tempo and keeps an edge on the science that is taught. Sadly, teaching is often the less respected of the two functions. Research grants bring money and prestige to the institution. Service to the student and the profession tends to be rewarded primarily with personal satisfaction.[1]

Teaching and research can be done well by the same individual but it may be necessary to build some firewalls so that the two don't contaminate each other. Research scientists who teach must avoid the natural tendency to herald their own insight as a beacon

---

[1] ...Generally in the afterlife

13

and to assign more historical significance to their work than it may merit.

Universities train our science professionals. According to the universities, they are doing a great job because there is a big demand for science professionals. This is a species of logic that is found only in higher education.

Those who hire scientists and engineers in the private sector are looking only for people who will *produce*. With your first job then, you acquire something far more important to future employment than an education. You now have a *previous employer*. All job applications have a space for this. Your new boss wants to know what your old boss thinks of your work and of course why he or she is now your *old* boss. It may be the only call that is ever made about you. If education is on the application at all, it simply says, institutions attended and degrees earned. What this means is, "Where did you go to school and did you buy anything while you were there?" In science, the degree is the credential that will get you that first job. It won't get you the second one. A scientist with impressive credentials, who is unimaginative and produces nothing, is expensive and useless.

It is entirely possible to earn an advanced degree in science that has only one dimension. There are big gaps in the general science education of some specialists. Maybe this is unavoidable, but we really should acknowledge it. You can have a Ph.D. in your own discipline and still be functionally illiterate in the opinion of your colleagues across the hall.[1]

The university system has evolved over many centuries. There have been many steering currents in its evolutionary course. It is naïve to think that this system has been carefully designed. It is most unlikely that the present structure of higher education represents the most perfect creation of the human mind. Those of us who have spent most of our lives in this world however, may sometimes come to believe that.

---

[1] ... or in some cases, your gardener

14

Since *we* have been anointed, we may perceive that the system works just fine. If the system selected us, then it must be a very good system indeed. If it has evolved an artificial and maladaptive selection process, we will be last to recognize it. If it is now selecting for a set of characteristics that are less than optimum, we who are among the chosen are not likely to point that out. Reform is rarely welcomed or embraced in higher education.[1]

The university adores the skillful, diligent and obsequious student. The true *scholar* on the other hand, can be a damn nuisance. They question everything, they challenge tradition, and they have an appalling lack of reverence for the established hierarchy of the system. They tend to value reason over authority They can be a disruptive and subversive influence on other students.

Some of our best minds are lost to professional science when they come to believe that the pursuit of science is minutia and meaningless academic exercises. What we get then are the survivors of the ordeal. These may not always be the best, the brightest and the most promising. They *will* likely be the most determined, disciplined and focussed. Well, that doesn't sound so bad, but are these really the *only* people we want in a field whose most valuable resources are new ideas and unconventional thought?

Sometimes it is possible to lose an idea in the structures we build to explain it. Ask a serious science student to explain some abstruse concept in his field and you may get a litany of learned responses and key words. You might not however, get an *explanation*. If you press for one, you may get hostility or condescension. We learn the answers sometimes without ever understanding the questions.

---

[1] The word "rarely" is used here to avoid the more inflammatory term "never." After all, I don't want to offend anyone. Fortunately university officials are generally unable to read footnotes in 8 point type.

Universities look at academic pedigree when they hire. There is a good reason for this. The science divisions have the minimum requirement that you know some science. This credential is absolutely necessary. Maybe you will be a genius in your research. Maybe, with time and experience, you will become a competent teacher, but that won't really matter if you have only superficial knowledge of the subject. It is entirely correct that universities place content background above teaching ability. Ideally of course, a professor would have both. A university education is expensive and the students are paying dearly for it. The knowledge is critical, but a few fundamental communication skills on the part of the faculty is not asking too much.

By the time a student reaches college we have to assume that a fair fraction of the intellectual burden will be shifted to *their* shoulders. What we want are highly motivated self-starters who don't require a lot of hand holding. A campus full of high maintenance, academically dependent students is hardly a desirable situation.

At the same time, the faculty is no place for shallow, intellectually threatened men and women who think that the lectern is a throne and that a teaching position is some sort of an award for having been a diligent student for a decade. These are the professors who seem to feel that university teaching is a contest of wits between the professor and the student. At some point the ability to actually prepare students in the content must become more important than taking academic scalps. The saving grace of our universities is that most professors outgrow this or they move along to other professions. Sometimes a wizened department head will gently counsel them and explain it thus:

Look, this is not about you anymore. It's about them now. You had your chance to dazzle us all when you were a student. It's their turn now, not yours. You need to quit crowing about how brilliant you were as a student and find out right now whether you can teach or not. You must understand that you fail if they do not surpass you. You don't impress anybody by trying to compete with your

16

students. You're supposed to teach them, okay? Not stand in their way like Cinderella's wicked stepmother.

... And oh, by the way, you take my parking space just one more time and I'll publish your home address and phone number in the Departmental Student Bulletin... you nit-brained, pointy-headed little sack of fetid fish guts!

Sometimes they leave that last part out of course, but they probably shouldn't. It sharpens the focus and reduces ambiguity. When it works, everybody wins, and when it doesn't, natural selection steps in and creates a new parking space.

Universities can do a much better job than is currently the norm. Science courses offered to the general population sometimes seem almost designed to alienate and disaffect. To put it bluntly, they are often deadly dull. In some cases they are little more than remedial high school courses built around the least interesting and most pedestrian tenets of what might legitimately be called science fundamentalism. Interesting and exiting science, it seems, is reserved for the "brotherhood."

If you need the science hours, you may have to take such courses. It is unlikely that your science literacy will be much advanced by the experience. Your education might be better served (and your money better spent) on a good science magazine subscription, but that is not one of your options. If such courses are a clever plot to arrest the development of the population at the middle school level in science, then it is working beautifully!

In those institutions possessing the courage and confidence to permit the practice, course requirements may be "challenged" by examination. Personally, I think I would prepare on materials from sources other than the campus bookstore, but it would certainly be worth the effort if you have the opportunity. Remember that they can't make these exams *too* hard, or their graduates couldn't pass them. ... And that, you see, would be a very *bad* thing.

Elementary Education majors, to cite one example, need a great deal more science content than they get now. Requiring them to take more hours of "glassy-eye science" will not help. Neither will another dozen hours of "science methods" courses. They need adult science content. What is needed here is a full-up redesign of the science divisions. They will all do this eventually when they have no choice, but a few brave and forward thinking institutions will have to blaze the trail and pave the way first.

This is just how it works. It takes great courage to change anything. Change in higher education requires Gandhi-like courage, with a little William Wallace thrown in. The good news is that there *are* men and women like that hiding out in our universities right now. When the time comes, they will act quickly.

Research Science

A good research scientist is creative. The best of them are creative and irreverent. The most important quality in scientific research is imagination. Albert Saint-Gyorgyi (1893-1986) was a Hungarian-born American biochemist. He was the first to isolate vitamin C and won the 1937 Nobel Prize for discoveries related to biological combustion. In describing the essence of research he said, "Discovery consists of seeing what everyone else has seen and thinking what no one else has thought."

Those research scientists whose names we find in science textbooks are always those who ventured outside the respectable and the accepted. There is no Museum of Great Replicators.

Science works like this: 1. You observe; 2. You record your observations. 3. You create a model that explains those observations in a coherent way; and 4. You communicate your model to other people. Modeling and communication are the higher functions of science. What real scientists do is *create*. Yes, that's right, they make stuff up. They don't just observe and record. Sorry if that's not the way you thought it was. Someone gave you some bad information I guess.

There is no reliable evidence that the "scientific method" that we all learned in school has ever been used outside the classroom. Scientists rarely admit to using it.[1] What they do is fabricate models to help us to communicate and conceptualize the world. Observe, collect, imagine, create is the usual pattern. A good scientist has a good imagination and is a good communicator. A great scientist has a great imagination and a gift for language.

---

[1] "I do not frame hypotheses." Sir Isaac Newton, 1642-1727

Human beings can't tolerate cognitive dissonance. If your behavior is in conflict with new information then you are going to have to discard one or the other. A real scientist leans toward accepting the new information. Sure, it might be wrong and the old model may be very attractive, but if it is right it may lead to something even better.

Some "respectable" scientists prefer to reject new findings because they are disruptive to the good order of the culture. They know that the only effective way to preserve *truth* is to protect it from the corrosive effects of new information. The old model may even be critical to the validity of some well-established and dearly held understandings. For this reason, many respectable scientists do not take incoming calls. They remain respectable and they write books, but they don't have books written *about* them

Old models may acquire the mantle of absolute truth. They can be very hard to kill. They are "patched" until they are mostly patches. Sometimes it takes decades, even centuries to topple them. Still, it is in no way a bad thing that science resists constant reordering. New ideas have to be demonstrably better than the ones they are replacing. A new model must pass grueling tests to depose an old one. One of the most important of these is predictive validity. If your new model accurately predicts the future behavior of a system and the old one failed to catch it, well then we have a winner. If it predicts "just as well" then it had better have some really neat diagrams or it's going in the also-ran category.

Simplicity is also good. The simplest explanation that satisfies all the observations is generally the best one. This principle is known as "Ocam's Razor." It was named for the British philosopher who published it. It was later replaced by an even simpler philosophical principle that works just as well.

For some inexplicable reason, we like to separate science and "the humanities." Science is a purely human activity. It is certainly one of the humanities if the other ones are. Gifted scientists are among the most creative people on the planet. It is a shame that this is not more widely known. Most accomplished scientists of my acquaintance are also to some degree, accomplished in the arts. They are musicians, painters, writers, and sculptors. Typically they are broadly read and educated. They are multidimensional people. They are very much unlike the nerd-in-a-lab-coat caricature. They generally appreciate history, art, music, literature and cartoons depicting scientists as nerds in lab coats.

It is currently fashionable in some quarters to segment human behavior into left brain and right brain functions. Scientists are presumed to be left-brained because they are rational, analytical, critical thinker types. Proponents of this dichotomy insist that one side of the brain is dominant over the other side. They hold that you must be either a left-brained person or a right-brained person. The dominant half of your brain, they say, determines what you are. People who say this are called half-wits.

In healthy brains, both of the hemispheres work collaboratively all the time. If one side of your brain really *is* dominant, then you are definitely *not* okay. As a matter of fact you very probably live in a very quiet place that has gates.

It is true that some scientists may have a few mild peculiarities. They can be weird. They don't *have* to be of course, but that's the way to bet. Unconventional thought is frequently accompanied by unconventional behavior. This makes them very interesting to other interesting people and really scary to dull people. The institutions in which they work quickly develop a tolerance for this quality or they advertise a vacancy in the position.

Among the strangest of scientists are those who prefer identifying themselves as mathematicians. Members of this category have been known to make stunning discoveries, not in a laboratory, but on a chalkboard or the back of a grocery list.

Theoretical mathematicians may even be annoyed at having their work labeled as "science." There is little need to placate these people as they are few in number and easily silenced by a Nobel Prize for Physics.

Engineering and Science

*E*ngineers are not scientists and scientists are not engineers. That is why there are different names for these professions. The following simple illustration demonstrates the difference between the two. Engineers solve problems and build things. For example, an engineer can build a wheelbarrow even though he or she may not understand the more complex physical and mathematical principles of the device. (There is a lot of physics and math in wheelbarrows.[1]) A scientist on the other hand understands all the physics and mathematics of the wheelbarrow but may have no earthly idea, which end *to pull.*

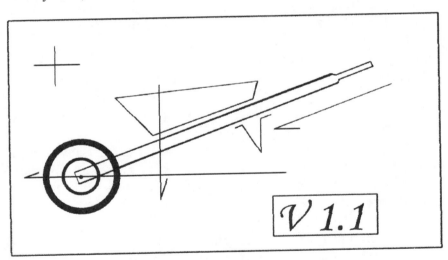

Engineers take lots of engineering courses in pursuit of their credentials. Engineering studies are sharply focused on specific materials processes and technologies. As a consequence, some

---

[1] The one-wheeled wheelbarrow was invented by French mathematician and physicist, Blaise Pascal in the 1600s. You thought I was just joking didn't you?

engineers are nearly innocent of science. A teacher with a license to teach secondary science has had more credit hours from the science divisions than an engineer has had. Please don't take my word for that. Look up the degree requirements yourself in any college catalog.

Engineers are valuable citizens and they serve critically important functions in our society. A scientist will not sit down and eat with one if it can be avoided, but they often work together on projects. Scientists and engineers typically see things very differently and they have a different set of values. Engineers *solve* problems and, if you ask an engineer, scientists *create* problems.

Scientists probe the mysteries of the natural world. Engineers typically design and build the systems and machinery that are used to do the probing. It might be better if scientists built these things for themselves, but unfortunately, they rarely know how to do that.

There is an unfortunate polarity that pairs the two sub-species in the most disadvantageous manner possible. The brightest and most skillful engineers are invariably forced to work with the slowest and most dim-witted of scientists, whereas the gifted scientist is inexorably doomed to be paired with the dumbest of engineers.

Were this not to be the case, you might well be reading this on the veranda of a sprawling cotton plantation on Mars. We can only speculate on how far we might have come, if ever at any time, a brilliant scientist and a brilliant engineer had worked together. According to the historical records of both communities, this has never happened.

To an engineer, there is a right way to do everything. To a scientist there are always questions about the way things *are*. They are different by training and culture.

Because they have the same chromosome number however, they may on rare occasions, interbreed. The offspring that do survive manage this by obtaining degrees in English Literature or by joining religious cults.

It has happened on occasion, that individuals *have* been trained in both disciplines. The resulting inner conflict leads straight to madness. This often manifests itself deceptively as a well-adjusted and happy state of peaceful intellectual strength and pleasant disposition. Because of this seeming normalcy, most of these individuals live among us, undiagnosed and untreated.[1]

The best engineers of course are the ones who push the envelope. While there are, in the various fields of engineering, some tried and proven formulas for approaching problems, there will always be new problems that confound the traditional methods. The ability to design and build a machine, a process, a material, or a system to do something that has never before been done, is a gift. This gift is the equal of any possessed by the brilliant research scientist. Nevertheless, some scientists are disposed toward looking down their noses at engineers. They may even trivialize the work:

> *"We have completed the complex theoretical foundations for an interstellar vehicle. All that remains now is the development of some very exotic materials, a propulsion system more efficient than any now in existence, and a way too keep people alive when you remove all their skin ... just engineering problems really."*

Sometimes the engineering "details" are more complex and challenging than the theoretical foundation.

When our species begins its migration outward into the solar system, there will be scientists and engineers among the settlers. We will need both, but unless we devise a better way to train them, it may be necessary to transport them in separate vehicles. These vehicles should carry no armament whatsoever.

---

[1] Archimedes, Greek mathematician, physicist, and engineer- 287 B.C.-212 B.C., probably suffered from this condition

25

Barbarian Science

Science and the Movies

Many times while watching movies on television, my children have shushed me with, "Come on Dad, it's just a movie!" Sometimes I can try to watch a science fiction film with the understanding that this is, after all, entertainment and not pedagogy. The trouble though, is that I don't really believe that! I think it *is* teaching and it may be orders of magnitude more effective and lasting than the science teaching going on at school. Some of us have gotten much of our science from the movies. Movie science is, I believe, getting better all the time. Still, while it may be more fun than real science, it is sometimes less accurate.

I will not name any specific films here. Everyone has their own favorite examples of science errors in movies and most of us enjoy discovering them and pointing them out to whoever is available as a demonstration of our superior knowledge. Some of us *cannot* keep from doing this, even if we try.

There is one that comes to mind in which there is a sunset with two suns of about the same apparent diameter and color. Now there are lots of binary systems in the galaxy. From one of the planets in orbit around *one* of them, you *could* sometimes see two "suns" appearing to set. The one you are orbiting however, should be very noticeably bigger than the other one. Ah, but what if the more distant one is much larger? Is it not possible that they might *look* the same size? Okay, sure, that's possible but not a good idea for an *inhabited* planet! The Earth receives about one two-billionth of our Sun's radiation. Another one close enough or large enough to present the same angular diameter in the sky is a problem that no rating of sunscreen will address.

Even in binary star systems, *stellar* distances separate the member stars. They are not that close, and in most cases the one you are *not* orbiting is just going to be a extraordinarily bright star, rather than appearing sun-like. The error didn't spoil the movie for me you understand. I loved it! It is actually a splendid teaching tool.

Some moviemakers are very particular about the science in their films and go to great lengths and great expense to make sure the science is sound and correct. They hire teams of science consultants to analyze every scene and every shot.

This does not mean that science teachers, scientists, and engineers will not examine every frame in slow motion to find some errors. To the scientifically inclined, this is the adult equivalent of an Easter Egg hunt. There is an unseemly, almost maniacal, glee associated with this activity.

Some errors are quite literally showstoppers. I have no trouble at all in strapping into the seat of a spacecraft that uses an imaginary mode of propulsion that does not now and will probably never exist. There are many technologies common today that were unthinkable to our ancestors or even to our parents. I have no trouble zapping unfriendly space monsters with hand held weapons of mass destruction that use the galactic magnetic field and the strong nuclear force as a power source. I can handle that, fiction is supposed to be fictional, but please, you cannot *go to* Ursa Major!

Ursa Major is not a place. It's a constellation. Constellations are *apparent* arrangements of *apparently* adjacent stars. They are only associated in our minds because they lie in the same general direction along our line of sight.

Go to another solar system in this galaxy and you will see a wholly different set of constellations. You will not however, see Ursa Major because it exists, only from here! The actual location of the constellation is the Earthling mind.

Perhaps our own Sun, as seen from a planet of some nearby star, it is part of some well-known arrangement. Maybe our Sun is central to a particular pattern of stars that is explicitly erotic or even pornographic to some alien mind! ...Well, it's just a thought, and it's not any sillier than traveling to some place that isn't a place. It is entirely possible, even likely, that there are constellations far less ambiguous than the ones we see from here.[1]

Movie vehicles can travel anywhere of course, but it really should be to a *where* and not to an illusion. Imagination venturing out from a position of understanding is good. Imagination from a misconception is really annoying. You have to know a little science to make science fiction.

A   **B**

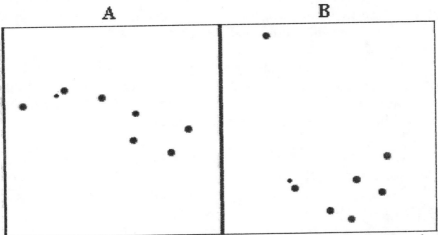

A portion of the constellation Ursa Major as seen from Earth, (A) and as seen from a nearby solar system. (B)

Science fiction movies have dealt very commendably with the awesome engineering challenge of interstellar travel. Many of these modes of transportation are plausible and well-reasoned even if wholly theoretical or whimsical.

---

[1] Okay, you need to stop thinking about that pornographic constellation now. We should move along.

Travel takes time and that can be a real nuisance in a ninety-minute movie. Getting Hero A to Villain Stronghold B while he is still in prime fighting condition and while Captive Princess C remains reasonably young and alluring, may require some shortcuts or even adjustments and alterations to the space-time continuum. You have to back off a little here. I mean, *it's just a movie.* Let them get to wherever it is they're going before you start picking. There are sure to be plenty of errors to find after they get there. For one thing, there are always the aliens.

What is wrong with most aliens in movies is that they are not nearly strange enough. It is very hard for us to create an alien species that does not resemble Earth fauna. We particularly like bugs and lizards because of their inherent creepiness. We are also fond of energy beings and artificial intelligence. They are almost always recognizable though and just a bit too familiar.

A real alien species, having followed a quite dissimilar course' of biological evolution, would likely be much stranger than anything we might invent. After we have actually *seen* some aliens, the movies will do a better job I think.

The movies have taught us an awful lot about the oceans, about animals, about space flight, medicine, engineering and a bunch of other things. In all seriousness, I do not think that school teaches science more effectively than a good movie ... or a bad one.

I am pretty well convinced that reading about snakes has less impact than seeing a really big one eat a village full of people. I am actually impressed with most of the science I have seen in movies and I do believe it is improving all the time. I think science movies, in general, are more faithful to science than historical movies are faithful to history.

Popular Science

*I*t would be difficult to identify the exact moment in human history when science became an exclusive brotherhood and a mysterious secret society. Presumably there was a time when anyone with a brain could engage in science. We all do it now of course but we are not to be taken seriously unless we are members of the inner circle. Science unfortunately has developed a priesthood.

The priests of science have gone through rigorous rites of passage. They have been draped with the mantle of worthiness. They have credentials. They have received advanced degrees in the exotic specialties and sub-disciplines of formal science. Having been granted a degree from a university, their words are often taken down and recorded, much in the manner of the Ten Commandments.

Everybody knows of course that some people with degrees are very smart, some merely have good short-term memories, modest academic talent and a great deal of time, and a few are actually dumber than a box of rocks. It is not likely that an unintelligent person will make a significant contribution to science, but it is verifiably wrong to assume that all persons with a Ph.D. in science are smart enough to cross a busy street unassisted. Unless you have been under house arrest for the last 400 years, you have met a few people who bore out this observation.[1]

---

[1]   Those who have been university students at one time or another, particularly those who have earned a Ph.D., have come face to face with the terrifying realization that we may be a species with no adult supervision.

Advanced science information has for many years, been closely guarded and kept from the riff-raff (presumably because they might *understand* it). Today though, with the proliferation of science information, it is only a matter of time until some unlicensed dabbler makes a pivotal and indisputable breakthrough. This used to happen all the time before science became a priesthood. It hasn't happened for a while now though, so when it does happen again, it may be traumatic. It will certainly be entertaining.

The late Dr. Carl Sagan was fond of saying that argument from authority is worthless. Authority can never be substituted for reasoned thought and scientific evidence. You can become an "authority" on anything by spending sufficient time and money at a university. But you become right by being... well, for lack of a better word, *right*.

Sometimes the "beginner's mind," unfettered by dogma, can make connections that the more disciplined and conventional thinker cannot manage. The best combination is the *well-educated* unconventional thinker, but "thinker" is the critical word in that sentence. In the history of science there have been significant contributions from undocumented workers.

Milton Hummason for example, was a muleskinner by trade. In the early 1900s, he was among the many workers transporting material and equipment to the peak of Mt. Wilson in California for construction of the 100-inch telescope. While on this job he became fascinated with the project and asked a lot of questions about telescopes. They probably were questions like: "What are you people going to do with this thing?" and "Why in the Sam Hill are you going to do that?"

He became entranced by the ideas associated with the telescope. He managed to land a menial job at the observatory when construction was finished. He decided to forsake his mules and explore the universe instead. He continued to learn, and because he was uncommonly bright, he came to know more than anyone

32

else about the peculiarities of the great instrument. He became the most highly skilled operator of the huge telescope.

Without a formal degree of any sort, Hummason became an accomplished, published and recognized Astronomer. He was a colleague of Edwin Hubble and participated in the discovery that the universe is expanding. He contributed to the development of a methodology to measure this expansion. It would be incorrect to say that he was uneducated. He was extraordinarily well educated and his teacher was Milton Hummason.

Today it would be hard for a muleskinner to gain entry into the halls where serious professional science is done, and that is perhaps the greatest weakness of our system. A man of lesser intellect with the right credentials could walk right in, occupy his space, produce nothing but memos, and remain employed for thirty years.

"Sure, Hummason made some brilliant contributions, but we just can't have muleskinners doing serious astronomical research! I mean, you let *one* in and there goes the whole neighborhood!"

Credentials are established to exclude from participation those who are not qualified. There is nothing wrong with this. Every profession must do this to protect its integrity. Evolving accreditation processes though, generally become more and more exclusive with time. As they become more restrictive, they become more specifically selective. As the portal narrows, the members come to be more and more alike in experience and temperament. In some fields, a degree from a *specific* institution is practically required. By the time this happens, the "guild" has poisoned itself. Divergent thinking has been filtered from that community and it is no longer alive.

There are many amateur Astronomers and not very many amateur Neuroscientists. Some specimens are just easier to come by. Science can be a very expensive hobby, and except for the very rich, it may require compromising standards and quality so that the phone bill is paid and the family dog does not starve.

There are very few amateur nuclear physicists because the toys are expensive. This is not such a bad thing. Some lines of research should perhaps not be carried out in garages.

Popular science may sometimes be superficial and shallow. It may lack the discipline and structure of formal science. That does not mean it is altogether invalid, just that it is sloppy and careless and lacks thoroughness. If it has genius behind it however, someone will come in to clean it up.

It sometimes happens that a brilliant amateur will recruit a card-carrying member of the scientific community to lend respectability to their work. The amateur may do all the thinking but the signature of an accredited scientist will "validate" the findings. There is not, in science nor in any other field of human endeavor, any substitute for brains.

Science *is* popular. Almost everyone dabbles in it to some extent. Even very young children engage in observation, experimentation and modeling for hours on end. They are generally undisciplined though and they almost always leave out the equations. For that reason, we don't name buildings after them until they are older and have done the math.

For the priesthood of science, the terror of the information age is that someone may pull back the curtain, like the little dog did in the Wizard of Oz. This is a very serious threat. It is easy to discredit and dismiss someone with no papers when they are wrong, but what if they are right and they can prove it and they have met all of your standards and filled in all the boxes according to the rules? What do you do then? If science is your profession, then you had better be really good at it. Professional science will have to thin its own herd soon or have it done by the rabble.

If popular science represents a potential threat of exposure to the "priesthood" of science, it is a valuable asset to the truly gifted and innovative scientist. The more people understand your work, the less likely you are to face an angry mob with torches and pitch forks. There is nothing harder than getting grant money from terrified peasants.

In April of 1990 NASA placed the Hubble Space Telescope in Earth orbit. This 2.4 meter optical telescope, circling above the Earth's atmosphere, has given us our first real look at the universe. Most of the images from Hubble are eventually available to the public on the Internet. Lots of amateur Astronomers and others have the opportunity to study these images. What if the pros miss something subtle but very significant in one of those images and a gifted eighth grader catches it? Well, that would just be great wouldn't it? Well, wouldn't it?

Popular science is generally good for professional science. It creates a more enlightened voter, a more enlightened investor and a more enlightened consumer. If the dilettantes occasionally go off on a wild goose chase, what's the harm? It just makes the professional scientist look that much smarter and, if they *do* come back with a goose, well then you just invite them in and offer to cook it in your official professional scientist's laboratory oven.

Occasionally a noted scientist will appear to court the favor of the masses. When this happens they are almost always excoriated by the brotherhood. Any attempt to popularize science is seen as giving the vestments of the priesthood to the congregation. It is a serious offense and the consequence is often banishment. The mere fact that some pompous individuals would decry the demystification of science and franticly condemn the offender, is alone, reason enough to do it.

Science *is* for the masses. Condescension has no place here and scientists who engage in it probably lack the necessary ego strength for the profession. The scientific community should advance popular science and nurture it. This is not just being magnanimous; it's also a lot safer.

Barbarian Science

Science and the Press

*P*erhaps it is possible that there are people who get most of their basic science information from science stories in newspapers or from radio and television news programs. If you are one of these people, then there is a good chance that you buy your groceries at a gas station and believe this to be the only place that sells food.

Journalists are not ignorant, uneducated or negligent people. I do not believe that reporting science badly stems from scientific illiteracy. I am sure that most newspaper writers are honorable men and women who genuinely want to convey the essence of any story to their readers as accurately as possible. Nevertheless, I rarely read a science story without hoping that I am holding the only copy of the paper that actually got to the street. Maybe through some miracle, the rest of the papers were lost or never delivered.

Science is interesting. People will read science stories. Some of these may have far-reaching social or political significance. They may be important news. Science professionals though, are sometimes baffled when a major story is not considered newsworthy and a pedestrian announcement of something entirely expected and predictable is offered up as a headline.

Among the more popular science stories are those from the fields of medicine, the environment and Astronomy. Look in any newspaper and see if you can't find at least one of these. They have great entertainment and personal interest value.

Among the Astronomy stories, "Scientists Discover New Planet" is a perennial favorite. For some time now we have expected to continue finding more and more evidence of planetary material in orbit around stars. Astronomers look for it and expect to find it and they do! Such discoveries are *very* significant and important to astronomers, but they are hardly shocking or surprising and they aren't really "news" for the general population. These planets of course are not in *our* solar system. A reasonably well-informed individual knows this and wonders why it is presented in large bold print.

To a newspaper, the best science story is one that is initially engaging, interesting and entertaining. That will not necessarily be the one the science community would have picked for the front page. Most U.S. newspapers carry a daily column on Astrology. Perhaps this should set off some sort of alarm. The Astrology column is classified as "entertainment" of course. Perhaps the science stories should be identified that way as well.

Scientists themselves must accept a portion of the responsibility here. There is apparently some unwritten rule that press releases from scientists must be torturously arcane and filled with as much technical jargon as possible. They seem to be written to impress colleagues. Naturally the paper has to edit out all of that complexity and convert this into something an eighth grader can and *will* read. In the process, they sometimes simplify the science right out of the story. Science types should consider their words carefully because if the reporter or editor doesn't understand it, there is little hope that the reader will.

Sometimes a simple misunderstanding can have a lasting impact. Our understanding of the natural world is based partly on observation and logic and partly on information we get from credible sources. When we trust the source, we place the stamp of truth on the information and we retransmit it to others as fact.

An orbiting spacecraft is under at least two strong physical influences. One of these is a result of gravity (g) accelerating the spacecraft toward the center of Earth at nearly 9.8 meters per second, per second. Another is the velocity imparted by a relatively brief burst of rocket propulsion (V). This thrust is at a tangent to the pull of gravity. The rockets are shut off as soon as the spacecraft has the necessary speed and direction. Inertia would then keep it moving in a straight line at a constant speed but the Earth's gravity bends its trajectory into a curved path.

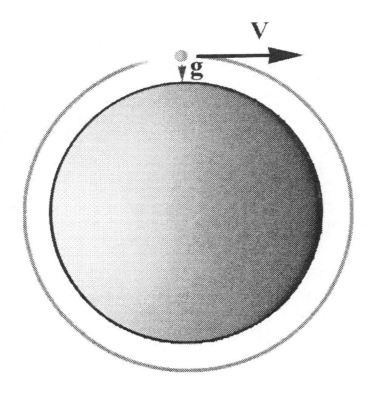

If V is great enough, the curved path will not intersect with the curved surface of Earth and the spacecraft will fall around the planet until acted on by some additional force. Because the spacecraft and its contents are falling along with each other around the Earth, you experience something that is very much like floating in the absence of gravity.

Isaac Newton explained orbital mechanics a few centuries ago. Sooner or later we will incorporate some of this into our culture and our education system, but we have not done this yet. In 1969 this nation landed men on the Moon. This happened while most of our population believed in the whimsical and quite erroneous idea that things don't fall if you put them in space.

You don't have to go into space to experience this floating business. You can experience free fall in an elevator. Go to the top of a tall building, disable the elevator's safety breaking mechanisms, get inside the elevator car and then have someone cut the cable. You will accelerate toward the center of the Earth at 9.8 meters per second, per second until you reach terminal velocity or run out of building. You will enjoy the experience of floating, as if weightless, until you reach the basement, at which time the experience will be over (along with all of your other experiences).

It is the same in an orbiting spacecraft. The difference is that in the spacecraft you are falling safely and serenely in a curved path *around* the Earth, whereas in the elevator, you are plummeting straight downward to certain death as punishment for vandalism. In either case the physical "feeling" is the same.

The seven original astronauts of the Mercury Program were all test pilots. Pilots have their own jargon. Pilots use the term "zero gravity" or "zero g" to describe the condition of free fall in an aircraft. They also speak of positive gravity and negative gravity. These are informal descriptors of an apparent condition. None of them exist in physics. An orbiting spacecraft is in free fall. Objects within it seem to "float" as if they were weightless because they are falling along with the spacecraft.

Certainly all of the original seven astronauts were well educated and had solid science backgrounds. They knew that 200 kilometers above Earth, the force of gravity is pretty much the same value as it is on the surface. They knew that they were not escaping the gravity of Earth and going to a place where there is no gravity at all. Still, they innocently threw the term "zero gravity" around and it appeared in news stories and interviews. The press picked up "zero g" and used it in practically every space story that was printed. Eventually most of the population of the United States, not to mention the rest of the world, believed, as an article of faith, that once you get above the atmosphere of Earth, there is no gravity whatsoever. To the press, zero gravity sounded like *no* gravity. That of course, evolved into matter-of-fact statements like, "There's no gravity in space."

This notion was quickly taken up across the culture. It was taught in the elementary and secondary schools and soon it became established dogma. People assumed that if it was in the paper and the astronauts said it, it *must* be right. After all, weren't these the smartest people on the planet? Isn't that how they got to be astronauts? Some teachers *still* teach this fallacy, even some physics teachers.

Had the original seven astronauts been English majors instead of pilots, they might have spoken more carefully. They might have said, "It is *as if* there were no gravity." That would have changed everything. It's such a simple thing, just a harmless aviator's idiom, but it is a very misleading and confusing term if you are not a pilot or an engineer.

After years of cajoling and whining from the academic science community, the astronauts finally stopped saying zero g and only occasionally lapse back into it during brief periods of cerebral dysfunction. The steady increase in the number of scientist astronauts certainly helped. Sure, it took twenty years of diligent nit picking, but even so, science educators should take pride. They were a lot more successful than the English teachers of the 1950s in their holy war against Dizzy Dean.[1]

Today we are building a permanent, orbiting laboratory that will be accessed and serviced by reusable vehicles like the Space Shuttle. Only a handful of people really have to understand how all this works right? Well, maybe that is true but since the real

---

[1] Dizzy Dean, for those unfamiliar with American history, was a baseball legend who pitched for the St. Louis Cardinals and the Chicago Cubs in the 30s and 40s. After his retirement in 1947, he became a sportscaster and covered baseball games on radio and television for CBS and NBC. He was 'a colorful character, born in the rural South, who was given to non-traditional usage of the language. He used such terms such as "slud" which he believed to be the past tense form of the verb, "to slide." Ole Diz was set upon by angry mobs of English teachers who believed that he was a terrible influence on children and a genuine threat to the integrity of the English language. They wrote letters to the networks protesting his abuse of grammar. He survived the onslaught and continued to contribute to the evolution of our language through the early 60s.

explanation is much simpler and makes more logical sense than the misconception, why not teach that to our children instead?

If we don't, then we will have to put up with impertinent third graders asking questions like, "If there's no gravity in space then what's holding the Moon in orbit? " or "Why doesn't the Space Shuttle just float off into some other part of the solar system?" Eventually, you have to answer them or they will mutiny, and anarchy can be particularly ugly among 8 year-olds. The fact is that there is not, in all of space and time, anyplace at all where there is no gravity.

No matter where you go in the universe, you will always be in overlapping gravitational fields. Everything in our solar system is gravitationally locked to the Sun and the Sun is gravitationally bound to the Milky Way Galaxy. Gravity is everywhere, including the inside of the Space Shuttle. It is as universal and pervasive as country music on AM radio.

Low Earth Orbit, (LEO) where the Shuttle operates, is not all that high up really. This altitude could be represented on a standard 30 cm. globe, as the thickness of a pencil. In this region, (only about 200 km above the surface) Earth gravity is almost the same as it is on the ground. The term zero gravity is hardly appropriate. Astronauts now use the term "microgravity" to describe the environment inside the Shuttle. This is accurate scientifically but perhaps somewhat unfortunate linguistically because it is routinely interpreted by laymen as meaning that at typical Shuttle distance from Earth's surface, there is only a tiny little bit of *Earth* gravity left. This is not the case at all.[1] To find a place where Earth's gravitational influence is "micro" (a millionth of a g), you have to go more than 6 million kilometers from Earth!

If you take a rock 200 kilometers above Earth and drop it, what will happen? Well, it will fall 200 kilometers in a fairly straight

---

[1] Around the Shuttle's center of mass there actually is a tiny little bit of gravity, which is not zero. This is not a function of the Shuttle's distance from Earth however. The shuttle is never far enough from the surface to make much difference in the force of gravity. With any orbiting spacecraft though, there is a small gravity gradient, in the case of the shuttle, about a millionth of a g.

line toward the center of mass of Earth. It will not just sit there, and it will not float. What it will do is immediately get about the business of doing what rocks do in that situation.

Ask this question to a selected sample of people. Be sure to include well-educated adults, teachers, scientists, engineers and an assortment of school children of various ages. The only ones who will consistently answer correctly are those in kindergarten! The rest of your sample is so contaminated that they will believe (based on authoritative sources) that sometimes when you drop rocks; they don't behave like rocks. Little children, unfamiliar with authoritative sources, will make rational predictions based on observation. They will also wonder why you asked such a silly question.

. **Shuttle Altitude**

Earth's Surface

There are many highly skilled and knowledgeable science reporters. These men and women carefully research and investigate the stories they publish and present. It is very difficult, even for these individuals, to be comprehensive in a sound-byte or to cover all the aspects of a story in limited column space. It is also unfortunately true that some reporters assigned to science stories may not possess the necessary background to grasp the essential elements and then condense and present the information accurately.

Print and electronic news media are an important part of our culture. By all means read the paper. Listen to the news and watch television. There is much there for your enlightenment and enjoyment. When there is a potentially important science story though, find out where it came from so you can investigate it later in more detail and with additional sources. Then you should go play baseball or do something with your children. This act will advance science literacy in America and human civilization in general.

Corporate Science

*I*ndustrial research is a rich field for spin-offs. Obviously, the quest for a better soap may lead to a more permanent ink, but it may also accidentally point to a cure for acne. "Impure" science often out-produces its uppity academic sibling and makes very powerful contributions.

Research is funded by governments, by grants from foundations or through corporate investment in development projects. Much of it takes place in universities and in national laboratories but there is a respectable percentage goes on in facilities attached to manufacturing plants.

It is certainly a fine and commendable thing that pure research having no clear profitability potential is funded and pursued. There have also been advances and discoveries from basic open-ended research that have lead to marketable results. The current flows in both directions.

Medical laboratories may carry on research that is directed toward the discovery of cures or treatments for specific conditions. Large foundations established to fight particular diseases often fund such research. Pharmaceutical companies, however, are in the business of manufacturing products that have exploitable markets. Drugs, treatments and processes that work will make money. It is common that serendipitous discoveries occur. A medicine developed for regulating blood pressure is found to have the side effect of stimulating hair growth. To the happy hairy beneficiaries, it matters little whether it originated from altruism or from energetic capitalism.

If you ask a random sample of Americans to identify two spin-offs from the U.S. space program, more than half of them may cite Velcro and Teflon. Wrong. Certainly the space program has profoundly impacted our lives and our economy and it has given us products, materials and processes that we use every day, but while a conspicuous user of both, it is responsible for neither Velcro nor Teflon.

Velcro was invented by a Swiss gentleman who became curious about how effectively burrs managed to stick to his clothing as he walked about the countryside. He wondered (in French) about the specific mechanics of this phenomenon.[1] One early use was by mountain climbers as a means of keeping all of their mountain-climber stuff on their belts. Teflon was developed, strange as this may seem, as a non-stick-cooking surface!

Manned space flight on the other hand is rarely credited with its development of the medical telemetry and monitoring systems so commonplace in hospitals today or with the current advanced communication-information technology that we take for granted. It would be hard in fact to find a place where you would be far away from space technology, even while cooking on the remote peak of a mountain.

Let us imagine that while pursuing development of a coating for the control surfaces of a high-speed aircraft, a worker is exposed to a certain chemical compound that is potentially dangerous. Appropriate safety procedures are initiated and the victim is treated for exposure to the chemical. A pre-existing condition however, requiring a particular drug treatment, has complicated the picture by rendering the patient uncommonly sensitive to the accidental exposure.

In this particular case, the heightened sensitivity results in a dramatic improvement in the pre-existing condition. Aviation

---

[1] Switzerland is an actual country even though it has no language of its own. The same circumstance applies to the United States of America, Mexico, Canada and a lot of other places. The deficiency does not appear to pose any sort of handicap to the citizens of these countries.

research has stumbled on an effective medical treatment that other researchers, dedicated to this problem, had been struggling with unsuccessfully for years. This is not so far fetched. Even less likely events have actually occurred.

In 1964, Arno Penzias and Robert Wilson discovered the cosmic microwave background radiation by accident while trying to eliminate noise from a huge microwave antenna. This happened at Bell Labs in Holmdel, New Jersey. For this discovery, they shared the Nobel Prize for Physics in 1978. It is one of the most important breakthroughs in modern Astronomy and it resulted from trying to build a better telephone. I have always wondered if either of them *really* thought of themselves as astronomers before that.

There is no reason to assume that corporate science will be less rigorous or less adequately funded than institutional science. In fact, it may be quite the other way around. Penzias and Wilson were not the first nor the last winners of the Nobel Prize to be employed in industry. Many corporations also support basic research even when there may be no obvious, short-term commercial applications.

The driver of corporate science is profit. Product research is undertaken to make money. Such research though, may require serious delving into the physics, chemistry, thermodynamics or biology of the associated systems and environments. Many of the materials, systems and hardware in medicine, communication, transportation and other fields were developed or discovered by private industry. A significant fraction of these advancements came from totally unrelated lines of research.

Some people may view corporate research as contaminated and tainted by greed. Perhaps it is viewed as evil because it is undertaken for money. Universities and other institutions I suppose do research purely for advancement of science and the public good. Maybe the money is just cleaner if it is not all tied up with profit. Oddly, we don't seem to mind using the products even if they *were* developed for selfish gain.

One reason for the high productivity of corporate science is that corporations don't retain unproductive workers. Natural selection is not suspended in the jungle of corporate research and the non-producer is as vulnerable as a crippled asthmatic antelope in a lion cage. Tenure and job security are alien concepts in this ecology.

Children's Science

*C*hildren engage in pure science. Observation, association and theoretical modeling are what we do when we are little. Even before we verbalize them, we have begun to operationalize theories about how gravity works, how sound travels and where light comes from. We have not yet been exposed to the centuries of science that brought us to this point in our history. We are innocent of its foundations. We invent the wheel. We discover fire. We formulate natural laws and we use them in our interactions with the universe. We are born scientists.

Formal science is typically introduced only after we get to school. We find out then that there is much that has been done. We begin to learn the language and structure of science. We learn that there are more effective ways to gather data than we may have used and that there are procedures that can save time or lend precision to our study. We learn that memory and first impressions are not always reliable and we learn to view systems in broader contexts.

We discover also that science demands mental discipline and that imagination alone will not answer all our questions. We are introduced to the intellectual stimulation of thoughtful inquiry. We discover that we have been given much by those who came before us. We cross the threshold and we are welcomed into the human community of science.

Okay, so that's *not* what happens, but it's what *should* happen. Maybe for some children in some classrooms, it does happen like that. If that is so, then we must do all we can to allow this accident to happen more often.

Science is so much a part of our healthy intellectual development that it would be tragic if it were stunted at an early stage. Suppose we came to school only to have our curiosity frustrated, our fascination with the natural world stifled and denied. Suppose that science was presented as a dull and sterile series of lists and memory exercises. Suppose that all we ever did was *read* about it. What would that be like? Well, it would be like... *familiar*, wouldn't it?

I used to long for summer. It was not just that I wanted to be outside, to be liberated from oppression, to cast off my shackles and breathe the clean air of freedom. It was more than that. I longed for summer so that I could learn.

Learning to me was more associated with solitude than anything else. I had a chemistry set. I had a lazy stream full of living, swimming, crawling, eating, reproducing "things." I had an attic room in which to perform hazardous and/or forbidden experiments and I had access to the sky. Most of what I learned was accidental and much of it was wrong but I wanted to be a scientist then. I was interested in everything.

School was my least successful experiment. I never really figured it out. I knew they believed they were doing something good for me and I could not understand how they managed to get it so horribly wrong. I was told that I was smart but that I was undisciplined, lazy and irresponsible. I also dimly understood that for some reason, they generally saw this as a *bad* thing.

We have all seen those cute lists of children's goofy answers to science test questions. Some of them are hilarious: "blood flows down one leg and up the other." "Thunder is caused when lightning hits a transformer." "The pornograph was invented by Thomas Edison." "The Nitrogen Cycle is why it is dark at nite." A paramecium is where baby meciums come from." What strikes me about these answers is not their abysmal "wrongness," but the stunningly logical thought behind some of them.

Without the faintest clue of what the right answer might be, these urchins have cooked up a fairly rational response, seemingly out of thin air. What they reveal is not a lack of understanding or a lack of intelligence, but merely a lack of information. And that can be corrected.

When we are quite small we begin to explore the universe. Science is our first purely human behavior. It begins before spoken language, before we begin to appreciate art or history or oral hygiene. We come to associate cause with effect, action with reaction. We discover for example, that when we crawl toward that thing that we have not yet learned to call "the heater," this invariably causes the sudden appearance of enormous feet. We test this hypothesis repeatedly and verify that the feet always appear when we draw to within a certain distance.

We explore Thermodynamics and discover that when we are cold, we can warm ourselves without assistance, but the phenomenon is transient. We learn to associate sound with motion and we discover both the principle and the joy of percussion. We perform experiments with gravity and inertia and suspect, just as Einstein did, that they may be equivalent since they sometimes

51

involve similar unpleasant sensations. We investigate the capabilities of our senses and determine that visual observation is interesting but more reliable data is acquired through taste. We don't have words for these concepts yet, but we form them in our minds. New laboratory equipment periodically and mysteriously arrives. We start looking for grants.

Piaget believed that the thinking of young children is concrete and not abstract. I simply cannot imagine why he thought that. I believe the opposite is true. I won't argue this because he himself is dead and his disciples are psychologists and I am unable to communicate successfully with persons in either demographic.

When I was very small I observed that all sounds have a visual component. They have shapes. The shape of the sun shields on some old style traffic signals for example, is a fairly close visual representation of a sound that is not unlike the vocalization of the word "California." Now before you ascribe this entirely to madness, be informed that I have encountered *others* who have noticed this relationship between solid geometry and sound. Our perceptions of these relationships are frighteningly similar. Some people see shapes in the world and we can hear them. There is even a sharp differentiation between the sounds of shapes in nature and those of human artifacts. I wonder what it means.

Children acquire information about the natural world through observation. They analyze these observations and conceptualize from them. Later, they begin to examine the work of earlier observers. They exercise critical thinking. They assess these earlier models and ideas and then integrate them into their own intellectual structures or reject them and continue working on alternate solutions. This continues until death or until they accept the idea that their own thinking is defective and the view of established authority is sacred and imutable.[1]

It would be unfortunate if our schools taught children that science already knows everything and that thinking is maladaptive. It would be equally sad if they taught us that all we should rely

---

[1]   Traditionally at about second grade.

solely on our own thinking and completely ignore our awesome heritage of scientific inquiry. I wonder if there are places where this happens.

One of the best teachers I ever had instructed us never to leave a question blank. "If you don't know the answer, then make something up," he said. "It could be right and even if it's not, what have you lost? I might even give you partial credit if you just spell some of the words right." Later, he would read the well-reasoned ones (and the funny ones) in class. I can remember actually looking forward to going to that class. I even did most of my homework. He did another remarkable thing too. He didn't teach *for* the test, he taught *with* the test. By that I mean that he used the test to teach us.

He asked lots of discussion questions and he seemed to be interested in learning how we thought. He loved the ideas of the science he was teaching us and he got excited when he explained them. He believed that creative thought and innovation were the most essential elements of good science.

He was also a coach, and by all accounts, not a very good one so he didn't stay very long. This was a good thing of course because it moved him around to different schools. He finally got out of teaching altogether because he couldn't string together a sufficient number of winning seasons. He was much respected though and he made a real difference.

The coach as poor teacher is a favorite stereotype in our culture. I have never been that comfortable with it myself because of that single example. I guess some coaches *are* poor teachers, but in my own experience there is at least one exception and that has been enough to invalidate the theorem.

Much earlier, I had sworn a solemn oath to myself that if I ever got out of the third grade; I would never set foot in another school building again as long as I lived. I had fully intended to honor that sacred commitment. I didn't seriously consider teaching until I had already been in college for a while. When I finally did consider it, the influence and example of this gentleman certainly made the profession less unthinkable.

Science Teaching

I am a teacher. That means that I am a member of the world's oldest profession. Yes, I know you thought that other service industry enjoyed that distinction, but actually we predate them by several centuries. The newer field opened up only when teacher salaries failed to keep up with the cost of living.

I am also a zealot and I represent the extreme radical lunatic fringe in education. I can see little in the present system that is worth saving. I am a proponent of radical, disruptive, painful, catastrophic change. In short, I am in favor of dragging the "temple" down. Back when I had long hair, I spent a lot of energy trying to get myself chained to the right pillar.

We have changed education but not nearly enough. Students are still advanced on accumulated time rather than through meeting standards of achievement and independent scholarship. The school day and the school year are essentially the same as they were seventy years ago. The basic systemic architecture is unchanged. We still value and reward passive participation over intellectual development. There has been some change but it is largely superficial and not all of it is good.

For example, "Discovery Science" is a wonderful thing. It is vital and necessary in science education but it is *not* sufficient by itself. Sometimes when a kid asks a question, you should just answer it. It is not necessary to make your children recreate the Stone Age in order to appreciate rocks. I will make a bold statement here: **Children are interested in science content.** They *love* it. They will even *read* about it when no one is watching. Sometimes they will ask us urgent questions and we will respond with, "Well, what do you think about that? How could you go about setting up an experiment to find the answer?" It is a good thing that we are bigger than they are because this triggers a primal attack response.

Yes, they need to conduct experiments and investigations. That is true, but sometimes they just really *need* information. Smart teachers, it appears, just *know* when to dispense it and when to send the child on a quest. Perhaps they know this because they have some understanding of the science involved.

It seems that in education we have never quite balanced the discovery-information equation. We tend to go way too far in one direction or the other. Science without substantive content is nothing more than fantasy and supposition. Real science is fascinating to children. Learning that is limited only to discovery (or re-discovery) isolates the student from the scientific achievements of the past. It disinherits the young. On the other hand, science gutted of its exploration, imagination and discovery, is child abuse. Learning that is based solely on memorizing transient "facts" is so dull that it can be intellectually lethal.

In an attempt to make science more friendly, it is now mandated in some schools that ALL science must taught with hands-on-activities. Now this may sound wonderful to some people, but it is not wonderful at all. If it were, then we would now have some fantastic test scores. Good teachers use direct experience whenever they can. They involve the learner with something other than the printed page. But *good* teachers are smart and they also engage the student with the ideas. To do that it is necessary that the teacher grapple with the content.

Science is fun and interesting all by itself. We don't have to make a game out of it to get children to learn it. Neither do we have to make a painful ordeal of it to make it valuable and worthwhile.

Apparently at some point, it was observed that good teachers do lots of hands-on. From that observation came the absolutely mindless assumption that if all teachers did that, they would get similar results. The *kind* of activity, the *purpose* of the exercise and the skill and knowledge of the teacher directing it, are all critical. It is a very powerful tool. It has long term effects. Therefore it should be used skillfully, or else rarely.

Discovery science has become the miracle elixir, a substitute for really *teaching* science. It has become the educational equivalent of the snake oil remedy. In the hands of a skilled teacher, hands-on science is the most valuable tool in the kit. In the hands of a mediocre teacher, it is worse than doing nothing at all. Not every teacher is bright enough or talented enough to teach science with laboratory experiences. Hands-on teaching is neither simple nor easily done. Encouraging everyone to do it all the time is not sound thinking. A poor teacher may conduct a completely pointless activity and then truly believe that, by that act alone, they have "taught science" today. Hands-on science that just kills time and *looks* like science is bad. No, wait, not *bad*, EVIL!

This is all moot of course. Actually, in most schools, it is of no consequence whatsoever *what* children do while they are there. The primary consideration is that they are there! The real bottom line is time. Sure we administer tests from time to time, but they are completely meaningless. If the test results *did* mean anything then they would certainly effect the time requirement.

Students advance from one academic level to another based primarily on **time in the system**. Teaching methods, teaching skill and learning ability may vary but the time does not. The school year is nine months long for everybody. Some will meet the standards and some won't. If we were really teaching to a performance standard the time wouldn't matter would it?

In the typical school system though, if you meet all of the standards but do not serve the required *time*, there is not the slightest chance that you will pass and advance to more challenging material. Have you ever heard of a student who had passing test scores but failed because of "inadequate attendance?" Yes, of course this is nuts and yes, this happens all the time.

And what if they *don't* meet the requirements? Well, we have a single solution for that problem. It is *more time!* We simply recycle them back through the system. They repeat the entire grade level!

If performance is the standard, then time will be a variable. If time is the standard then performance will vary. In the typical school performance does vary. Typically it varies all the way from adequate to inadequate. There are educators who will seriously defend this absurd practice as if it made some sort of sense. There are also many that recognize its intrinsic stupidity but are convinced that it is impossible to change it! Any reorganization, it is presumed, might disturb some delicate cosmic balance.

It's as simple as this. You can advance through grade levels or you can advance to performance standards. If you really think you can use both to measure student progress, then honestly, you need to sit alone in cool dark place and think about this very carefully for a long time. Clearly, you have been badly damaged by radiation or something.

If the goal here is to raise the bar for every student, then you use performance standards. If the goal is to keep the system alive and growing then you use lock-step grade levels with advancement based on time in the system. That is what we have now in most cases. The prevailing system works well only for a specific subset of the student population. Neither the nine-month school year nor the K-12 grade level structure is founded in research. It just evolved that way. Twelve consecutive packages of curriculum, nine months in length and sub-divided into days of fifty minute periods has never had any particular validity. Actual people don't learn in that arbitrary pattern.

According to general systems theory, large systems eventually take on the characteristics of a living organism. They maintain equilibrium, they continue to grow and they resist the introduction of anything that is identified as "not self." There may be many bright people within the system who would like to change it, but at some point it takes on a "life force" of its own. It maintains homeostasis, it grows, it produces fractal reflections of its organizational structure and of course it *eats*. Unfortunately, this particular system eats children.

Would you fly on an airline that boasted a 80% safe landing record on all domestic flights over one hour? Well, of course not, but you might choose to send your children to a school with a 40% failure rate if they have top accreditation rankings because of an excellent teacher pupil ratio, plenty of computers and a really modern bus fleet.[1]

The sad truth is that if *our* children are doing well, we don't really care what happens to the rest of them. When we *do* want to help, it often takes the form of helping other people's children become more like *our* children so they can succeed.

We have come a long way in education and we have made some progress. I wonder though, if we can progress much further without radical change in the present system. Well, okay, I don't wonder about that at all. But I am trying to get *you* to wonder about it.

---

[1]   This analogy has been often used by the Italian-born American anthropologist and archaeologist, Marco Giardino. To my knowledge, he has never owned a restaurant.

What constitutes an acceptable failure rate

Standards are a wonderful and insidious idea. The system does not recognize the threat that this idea represents. It mimics "self" so it is not rejected. How can the system oppose the idea of standards? It slips right past all the defense mechanisms. It invades the internal organs and starts to eat away at the spine of the beast. It will eventually destroy it but we will have lost nothing and our children will have something much better.

Speaking of the children, it will become necessary eventually to involve them in the evolving development of educational standards. We cannot trust this entirely to them of course, they do not have all of the necessary background. Sooner or later though, it will dawn on us that neither do we. Every generation believes they are creating the future for their children. They never are of course. The future is designed by those who plan to live there.

Our children will intuitively know some things that we will not know. We can prepare them up to a point but in some ways they are better equipped to speculate on the future than we are because they imagine themselves in it.

Their perspective is different, just like ours was different once. We knew some things our parents hadn't guessed, and so do they. We should listen to them. Not *believe* them certainly, but listen anyway... because they are listening to each other and the future is being plotted out in small chairs close to the ground, not in teakwood paneled conference rooms. The real trick is in knowing when to pass the baton and get out of the way. Maybe that is the ultimate test of intelligence. I hope we pass it.

Barbarian Science

Ancient Science

*W*e didn't get "here" by good luck. The ancients were stunningly brilliant and accomplished in science. One of the meanest insults we have ever visited on our ancestors is the suggestion that everything they built was with the help of aliens!

Sometimes we are arrogant about our scientific accomplishments. We may prefer to elevate ourselves by standing on the necks rather than the shoulders of our giants.[1] We know the folly of this but we do it anyway. Thousands of years ago there were people on Earth who knew a lot more science than many of us know today. The reason we call today's work "modern science" is that the present era contains our birthday. Our science will be expanded and overwritten by our children. Count on it.

Ptolomeic science held that the Earth was the center of the universe and everything revolved around it. This view was accepted and taught for nearly two thousand years. This did not happen because the people of that era were stupid. The model that Ptolemy created in 100 AD is brilliant. It explains the apparent motion of objects in the sky and accurately predicts their changing positions.

Considering the technology utilized, the observations from which it was derived are remarkable. The model we use today is actually simpler than Ptolemy's model and it works more precisely. It is not so much that ours is right and his was wrong. It

---

[1] Isaac Newton acknowledged his predecessors with the following line: "If I see farther than others, it is because I stand on the shoulders of giants."

is much more accurate to say that the one we use now is more complete.[1]

The Aztec calendar was a sophisticated tool and according to some Anthropologists, it may have been used and reasonably well understood by a broad segment of that population, and not just the priest class. Our ancestors in Egypt, China, Greece the Middle East and the Americas were the same species as we. We are not biologically or intellectually different from them in any significant way. Our brains are the same size as theirs with the same number of neurons and the same number of potential connections and pathways. What we have that they did not have, is a longer genealogy and a richer legacy of evolving scientific thought. We know much of what we know because of what they left to us. We have extended and refined their work, rather than erased or supplanted it.

Ironically, we have also at times had to repeat much of what our ancestors accomplished because of our unfortunate tendency to destroy the work of our predecessors. For example, the first powered flight by a heavier-than-air craft was actually logged in Mongolia in 1887. This feat was accomplished by the great physicist and inventor...

Well, okay... so I was making that up, and I cleverly stopped before I had to invent a believable sounding name, but if it *had* been that way, there's a fair chance the records could have been destroyed. We seem to have a perverse need to do that periodically for some reason.

The journey to Mars began many centuries before we knew that Mars was a world. We built the Space Telescope as much for Archimedes, Aristarcus of Samos and Johannes Kepler as for

---

[1] The great Archimedes –mathematician, physicist, engineer and accomplished gardener who died somewhere around 212 B.C. - is responsible for some of humanity's most important breakthroughs in mathematics, science, technology and grapes. Some scholars believe he may also have subscribed to a heliocentric (sun-centered) concept of the solar system. Considering what we *do* know about him, this seems entirely possible. This possibility may cause us to wonder about other ideas that may have been misplaced.

Edwin Hubble. And they would have loved it wouldn't they? They would be very proud of us!

Our transition from terrestrial caves to space stations in low Earth orbit covers an insignificant span of cosmic time. In orbit, we are sometimes no more than a few hundred kilometers above the caves in which our ancestors were born. We carry within us a genetic heritage that goes back a long way. The Neanderthals were our neighbors but not *our* ancestors. We shared the planet with them for a while but they were never on the tenure track. When the last Neanderthal left the planet he didn't turn out the lights. He also left to our stewardship the spare parts from a genetic past we shared long before we came to that fork in the road that started us down the path to Astronomy and information theory while he strolled off into Paleontology.

I have this fantasy in which I am transported back in time and permitted to meet and communicate briefly with the very first of our knuckle-dragging, barely human forebears. No doubt there are others more worthy than I to represent our epoch, but this is *my* fantasy. They should have thought of it.[1]

What I'd want to do is tell her that we "did good," that our species survived, at least so far, and we learned an awful lot in a relatively short time. I would say that it was tough in spots and we nearly lost it all a few times but hey, we did alright really.

"Those big cats, you know, with the huge teeth, well, they all died!" (At this point I smile and nod and extend a thumb upward from a closed fist.)

"And guess what, we learned how to build bridges that don't break in the middle, and how make fires without banging rocks and we invented clothes that don't smell like rotting animal flesh. There's a bunch of other stuff too but it would take kind of a long time to explain it and I can see you're pretty busy what with

---

[1]   Maybe they did but the records were destroyed.

65

getting food and not becoming food and such, and a lot of it wouldn't make much sense to you I'm afraid."

The furry precursor looks puzzled now but is neither afraid nor hostile.

"I just wanted to let you know, it's ... okay. Things got better. We turned out well. And I just wanted to say thank you. You gave us a good start, and we appreciate it. I know it must have looked pretty hopeless to you sometimes from back here. You never knew if your kids were going to live long enough to reproduce. Well, they did and things went pretty well, and way off up there in the future, we think you were pretty cool!"

We exchange some basic primate non-verbal communication and I take my leave after an awkward high five slap that produces a small cloud of dust from the aforementioned knuckles. Our ancestor is still baffled but strangely comforted by the visit and walks away a little bit more erect and thinking, *Hey, this feels pretty good ... and I can see a little farther too.*

Science and Religion

Science and religion are different functions but there is plenty of room for both in the normal human brain. If the two of them are not getting along in your head and the struggle is keeping you awake, then you may have to separate them.

It is possible that we are "hardwired" for the human religious response. It may be rooted very deeply in our brains. There are thousands of formalized religious groups and innumerable personal religions. Even those having no theology at all will sometimes express a kind of spiritual or philosophical self.

I have known many scientists. A few were Atheists but most of them practiced some kind of religion. They were Presbyterians, Jews, Catholics, Moslems, Hindus or "something elses." I have not encountered a single one who was tortured by internal conflict or who had the slightest trouble accommodating their occupation in their religious philosophy.

Science has never intentionally trod on the toes of religion but historically, they have locked horns on a few issues. Religion is based on faith. Articles of faith are accepted without question. Science is intrinsically a questioning business and you can't really engage in it if you already have lists of acceptable and unacceptable answers. Problems were bound to arise I guess, but thankfully we seem to be outgrowing most of them. At least we have dropped decapitation as one of the standard arguments. Some may lament this because it was a very powerful argument, and it always produced a profound change in thinking.

If your religion requires validation by science then it probably has no legs of its own. If you are thrashing around for "supportive evidence" then the "faith module" of your religion is not working. If your scientific inquiries have their outcomes predetermined by your religious convictions then they are not, even by the most generous of definitions, scientific. Please don't expect the rest of us to take you seriously. We might try to be polite but we will be scanning the room for exits all the time.

Science and religion operate in different realms. They don't really overlap because science deals strictly with sensory inputs while religion can, and in fact *must*, operate independent of them.

According to the Bible, God created the world in six days and then on the seventh day, he rested. Scientific examination of the evidence indicates quite unambiguously that the universe has been evolving for billions of years. If, in your mind, this means that that religion and science are in conflict, then I guess you are going to have to choose one and throw the other away. That's a tough break for you because you may really need both of them. We're all really very sorry about that. Honestly.

On the other hand if you think it merely represents two internally valid but different perspectives on the same reality, then there's no problem. If you do try to make them converge and agree on every detail then you are probably going to wind up with defective versions of both. Thank you for not sharing them with us. Good luck to you.

Science doesn't speculate on why there is a universe or what purpose it serves. It also does not have any position on the existence or personality of God. Of course it wouldn't. Science is a human activity, carried out with human senses, human brains and producing human explanations. It doesn't claim to be anything else. The intersection of the planes of religion and science lies primarily in language and not content. Allow me to illustrate.

When I was about nine I was wrestling with several thorny theological issues. One of them was this: If God is all-powerful and he created the universe, then certainly he could do this instantly, with no elapsed time whatsoever! I could not see why

The Creator of the Universe would take *six entire days* to do this job. And then he *RESTED?* ...Excuse me? GOD...*was tired?* Surely God does not get tired!

Six days seemed like an excessively long time to me. Maybe it's not so long to an adult, but six days is darn near a week to a nine-year-old! How could it possibly have taken *that long?* I mean, we're talking about God here, and how can we believe that he had to rest? Why would he fritter away six whole days and wear himself out on a project that would take no time at all? By the time I was eleven, I had an answer that satisfied me, so I stopped thinking about it.

Galileo was brought before the Holy Inquisition in 1633 to answer charges of uttering the heresy that the Earth revolves around the Sun and not the other way around. The inquisitors were completely justified of course. Before Copernicus and others articulated the heliocentric theory, the Sun, Moon, planets and stars actually *did* go around the Earth. As soon as the theory was uttered however, the universe instantaneously reordered itself and snapped into its present configuration.

God, in the opinion of some, was livid at having his work edited by man and retaliated by visiting a variety of plagues and pestilence on the human race. After a while though, he decided that he liked the new way better and he relented. The news of God's change of heart did not reach the religious establishment for centuries. To them the universe itself stubbornly remained in contempt. Galileo remained under house arrest and lived out the rest of his life trying to atone for having inconvenienced and annoyed God. He died in 1642 without ever getting the slightest bit of credit for helping The Creator get things right.[1]

This is a complete fabrication of course. God, it seems, rarely communicates with theologians at all. Perhaps this is because he

---

[1] Actually God never issued any detailed public statements on the architecture of the universe. Man just assumed that he would be located at the center of everything and added that part on himself. When Galileo suggested otherwise, it was of course, the theologians and not God that he was challenging. Theologians frequently have trouble making this distinction. The line between taking God seriously and taking themselves seriously becomes fuzzy sometimes.

cannot get a word in edgewise. When he does communicate with them, it is almost always late. For example, they still have not been informed of the latest revisions to the Fourteen Commandments.[1]

From a scientific point of view, human beings are a single step in the local evolution of the cosmos. It is equally possible that from the religious perspective, "modern man" may not be the final masterpiece of creation.

Religious thought has changed a great deal over the centuries. Although the words in the various sacred texts remain unchanged, there have been new understandings and interpretations of the writings. As our culture changes, so do our religions. The fundamental moral principles still serve us and nurture us as they did in the past, but theology evolves. We need neither to scrap religion for science nor science for religion. That would make little sense. They serve different functions and answer different human needs.

Perhaps we would do well to remember that religion, like science, is practiced and pursued by human beings. It is then, from time to time, subject to similar human foibles. Religion practiced by deities would be much more refined, although such behavior would be somewhat difficult to explain logically.

---

[1]   There are only ten. I just said that to mess with them a little.

Science and Politics

*L*awyers have discovered science. With any luck scientists will notice this before too long. Legislation regulating and restricting research is an important social and moral issue. Unfortunately, decisions on these matters may be made by people who are living on a flat Earth, crawling with leprechauns and vampires.

It is not inconceivable that the electorate may be one day faced with a critical decision on a matter of science. Environmental issues are particularly emotional and with good reason. Decisions on such issues may be critical to our survival. Those who best play the politics of the situation may very well prevail. A political decision may be made that has far-reaching scientific impact. If it is politically correct but scientifically wrong, it could be most unfortunate.

There was a small planet once, not far from here, which was inhabited by a pleasant and congenial species of marginally intelligent beings. They had, relatively early in their history, developed an advanced global social and political system based on true democracy. There was little crime or disorder and social unrest was very rare. All issues were decided by referendum of the citizens. There was universal suffrage and all had a voice in the decisions. They had long ago separated science from the masses and confined it to a small trusted and revered group of elders.

One day, these practitioners of science discovered that a giant asteroid had assumed a collision course with their world. When the news was released, there was much discussion on how catastrophe might be averted. There were many impassioned speeches. Either the asteroid's course must be changed or they must evacuate the planet and seek accommodations elsewhere.

71

The issue was put to a vote. The population decided
overwhelmingly that a change in the asteroid's course would be
best. Having voted then, and being absolutely confident in their
system of government, they naturally assumed that the best
possible course had been selected. The government was directed
to change the course of the asteroid. They would no doubt be safe
from harm. Unfortunately for the electorate, asteroid course
changing technology lagged considerably behind progress in
interstellar fight. The result was natural selection on its grandest
scale and lots of parking spaces.

If we, on the Earth, should face an environmental issue of grave
consequence, we might debate it in worldwide forums of
government. The course of action might easily be decided through
political processes. Reputable scientists on all sides of the issue
would be heard, but there is every likelihood that the case would
be decided on other than purely scientific considerations. If some
particular human behavior was adjudicated to be threatening to the
biosphere, it might be stopped, and if another were to be held

harmless by the courts, it might continue. If either course happened to have disastrous consequences they would still nevertheless be entirely legal and maybe even popular!

When scientists disagree (which is all of the time) then science issues are settled by public opinion or by the opinions of elected representatives. This only becomes scary if the population and its representatives are ignorant of science. What does one do when the experts cannot agree? If there is a very big gap between the population at large and the leading edge of scientific thought, then there may be problems.

We may not have reached that point yet however. As long as you don't see headlines on the grocery store tabloid racks with stories like, "Scientists Find Planet X" or "Alien Advisors on President's Staff" or "Minotaur Born to Detroit Couple," there's nothing to worry about.[1]

When we make political decisions on scientific issues we do not always base these choices on the preponderance of the evidence. Sometimes we may be tempted to select only the evidence that supports our position.

This is acceptable behavior in politics but it is indefensible in science. A scientist who attempts to make a name for himself by pontificating on some emotionally charged issue will inevitably incur the wrath of his colleagues.

Nuclear power is a volatile issue. There is no single, unified scientific position on the use of nuclear power plants. There are scientific positions supporting their use and scientific positions warning that the risk outweighs the benefits. In Nuclear politics, selective data gathering is blatant. This is always done by the *other side* however and not by your group. When so-called "scientific evidence" is cited, it is rarely done with any attempt to fairly present both sides.

---

[1]   Worry.

73

A scientifically unsophisticated public then might listen to the side that was shouting the loudest or to the side best representing their economic interests. A scientifically unsophisticated public might even be swayed by the views of well-known celebrities or performers... Well, no, that's preposterous isn't it? Nobody would be that simple. What was I thinking?

A good general rule is whenever you hear the words, "scientists say," you can be sure they didn't. Frequently you can substitute with: "This *One* scientist, well he *might* have been a scientist, said something, or at least is *reputed* to have said something, that sounded sort of like this." The phrase, "Scientists say" almost always precedes a lie. Scientists are a very very diverse group of people and *they* never say anything with a single voice. There is of course that one exception, "Ladies and gentlemen, my colleagues are wrong!"

Science and Economics

*T*he top two exports of the United States are science and agriculture. The world buys much of its science and much of its food from us. This is a big business and a big reason for the wealth and power we now enjoy.

If some of us are less than literate in science, then we are more or less gurgling morons when it comes to economics. That is hardly surprising. Particle Physics is dirt simple compared to economics.

Classical economics is a well-established and respected social science. It analyses mysterious forces and predicts the behavior of buyers and sellers and markets. Modern economics however, was invented a few years ago by a very small and extremely peculiar group of people who may or may not be of Earthly origin. I did not understand the older economics very well so I have little chance of understanding on any sort of level, how markets work today.

A few years ago some Americans were bashing a particular Pacific Rim nation for cutting into some of our markets. This was seriously counterproductive, because at the time that nation was also our second largest customer. If we protected our markets for U.S-built VCRs, for example, we risked diminishing the buying power of a major customer for other products. Calculations indicated that the more VCRs that other country sold here, the lower would be our individual mortgage payments. This of course would translate directly into lower unemployment figures, modest up-turns in beef production, increased low-end micro-electronics productivity, and higher prices for domestic strawberries.

Furthermore, it seemed for a time that our government might even have to consider subsidies to imported VCRs in order to prevent the resulting consequence of huge increases in American dependence on foreign oil, inflated prices for imported coffee and bananas and heavy losses in domestic poultry. This is very complicated stuff and involves planes of mathematics that are unknown to science.[1]

American science is among the most prolific producers in the world. We export science and food because there are hungry markets for both. Somehow they are also inexorably interrelated. There are mind-numbingly complex issues here. If we sell to another country a process or a technology that enables them to out-produce us in the open market then, this is bad, right?

Well, no, it's not because if we *don't* sell it to them and they buy it elsewhere or develop it themselves, then we forfeit the profit from that export which could have funded more expansion and further advanced development.

Perhaps the most baffling principle in the dark art of economics is that the richer everyone gets, the richer everyone *else* gets too. We don't want poor customers; we want rich customers because rich customers can buy more of what we are selling. We can make them rich by buying a lot of their stuff and by selling them stuff that makes it possible for them to make more stuff. I realize this is complicated. It can be more simply expressed by Einstein's familiar equation from Special Relativity: $E=MC^2$.

The equation is directly transferable to what is called Relativistic Economics. Energy (in this case wealth) is equivalent to Mass (stuff) multiplied by the square of the speed of light. In short, a very small amount of stuff can be converted into a humongous amount of wealth. You do this of course, by moving the stuff around. Einstein foreshadowed this in his General Relativity by stating that: The laws of nature are the same for all

---

[1] ... and possibly to mathematics as well.

uniformly moving systems. The concept was also alluded to centuries earlier in Isaac Newton's Principia Mathematica in the statement: An object in motion tends to remain in motion until acted upon by inflation[1]

How is it that we may give up major consumer markets to foreign producers and still remain the greatest of world economic powers? It is because we export science information and import heavy, massive objects. Mass and energy are equivalent in the relation expressed by the equation. Greater mass yields exponentially higher energy.

According to information theory, information is energy. If we export information (which has a rest mass of zero) and we import a very large amount of physical mass, (For example, automobiles and refrigerators) then we become richer. Because the total mass of our combined import product is greater than the amount of mass we export, (we don't count food exports here, food is really energy anyway) we gain mass and therefore exponentially greater wealth as a function of the equation.

We export information (at enormous profit) on how to make heavy objects and then we buy these objects from the countries that produce them. It's beginning to come together for you now isn't it? (Just say yes.)

The worst case for the global market is thermodynamic equilibrium or the heat death of the economy. This condition exists when mass-energy is uniformly distributed throughout the market. Emergency mechanisms are now in place to prevent this occurrence.

Although very effective, the least desirable of these mechanisms is war. If two producers possess roughly equivalent amounts of stuff, then the relief valve of war becomes a very real threat. Moving massive quantities of heavy material rapidly to other parts of the world may relieve the condition by tipping the balance and

---

[1]   This is not *exactly* what Newton said, but it is clearly what he meant.

reestablishing the energy flux. Many potential armed conflicts have been prevented in this manner.

If any parts of this explanation seem whimsical or strained to you, I can assure you that it should make every bit as much sense to you as any you might get from an economist. Relativistic Economics is new, but it is internally logical and sound. It has been thoroughly tested and verified to be at least as reliable as reading the Wall Street Journal ... or the entrails of an owl.

The best advice to rational persons on the subject of economics is to place your trust in the experts. No doubt this trust will be misplaced, but you will *feel* better, and when you feel better, that is good for the economy. When we worry about economic matters we run the risk that our attention may collapse the waveform of probability upon which the system depends.

In this same regard it is important that we never question the judgement of economists. It is necessary that they have unshaken confidence in the positions they have taken. It's sort of like when the coyote runs past the edge of the cliff but does not fall until he realizes that he is in midair. Economists *never* look down.

Science and Art

*I*n all art, there is science. We have to grapple with the science before any craft is elevated to an art form. To do a thing artfully, we must first master the science of that medium. The science of brushes and pigments or of sound or of stone or clay... or language lies like an iceberg beneath great works of visual art or of music, theater or literature. Artists manipulate sensory energies to communicate an idea. Every artist is a scientist to some degree. Those scientists who have achieved greatness are those who have elevated the toolmaker's craft to high art.

Humanity's truly great scientists were complex, multi-faceted people. Throughout history they have created for us the semantic, mathematical, schematic and graphical models that we use to conceptualize the universe and to communicate these ideas to each other. Ideas do not last very long without a host organism. I wonder how many we have lost over the millennia.

When science is constrained or regulated by some authority, when it is filtered by politics or religion or public opinion, we may risk losing something. The ceiling of the Sistine Chapel is a work of art. So is Hubble's Law. Both are creations of the human mind. It would have been so easy to repress either of them if they had offended some power or another. How different would we be without these two works? How different *are* we without the ones that we *have* lost?

Our ancestors were not, in any significant way, intellectually inferior to us. Mentally they had the same capacities that we possess today. Scientific thought is cumulative and evolutionary. It thrives on multiplicity and diversity. It stagnates when it is starved or bound. Perhaps there is some risk today that the institution of science will commit this felony upon itself.

Authority is no substitute for brilliant insight. Credentials cannot pass for creative intellect. Science is for all those who may be called to it. Today there is bad science, complex science, junk science, naïve science, advanced science, simple science, deep science, shallow science and pseudo-science. Who is wise enough to know the difference in advance of a breakthrough?

Right now, your opinion is as valuable as anyone else's but it will be better if you have more information. The most baffling challenge the universe has ever presented us is the understanding of ourselves. I am not at all convinced that there are as yet, *any* authorities on human behavior. Possibly, there have not yet been enough humans for a statistically significant sample. After all, we don't know how many of us there are *going to be*.

A chicken wakes up in a brand new world every day. They don't seem to retain much of what they learned the day before. Most of us aren't like that. We are able to build, not only on our own experience, but that of our forebears as well. We are not born with occupations and avocations as presets. We can understand and appreciate a very wide range of ideas and activities.

There is no physical difference between the capacity of your brain and that of a Nobel laureate. What makes the difference? Is it training, education, aptitude, imagination? Maybe it is all of these and maybe it is something else. However it may be, it is much too early to fence off the sciences and allow only a small segment of humanity to graze. We cannot risk that.

The great library in Alexandria was destroyed by a frightened and scientifically illiterate mob. If that mob convenes again, it may be huge and unstoppable. Science is too important to entrust to a small and arguably "elite" fraternity. Specialization, as Robert Heinlein said, is for insects.

Come up with a reasonable theory, model or construct that explains something in nature, and if it is simpler, clearer or predicts better than the one in common use, then it will make no difference at all whether you are a trained scientist or an accountant. There is no substitute for brains.[1]

The separation of the arts and sciences leads directly to the idiocy of forcing children to choose between the two. It happens that guidance and career counselors will sometimes steer high school students in one direction or the other. They seem hell-bent on channeling the creative child into non-science fields and only the highly structured and traditional students into science. Most of the students who are strongly encouraged to pursue science are those who have excelled at being *science students*. They are but a portion of those who might excel in research or engineering.

Aptitude in high school academic areas is no stronger indicator of associated career success than are hobbies or reading interests. How close did *your* high school counselor come to identifying your ultimate career choice? What about the people sitting next to you? Go ahead, talk among yourselves...[2]

Some children who excel in science courses in school do not make good scientists or engineers. There is substantial difference between the nature of the work done by science professionals and the nature of the activities undertaken in most classrooms. On the other hand, there do seem to be an awful lot of professional scientists who were in the band. There are even cases of individuals who demonstrated no interest or aptitude in science whatsoever while in school, but came to their profession as adults.

Maybe the selection process is flawed. Maybe we shouldn't have one. When you hear kids say that they "hate" science, you have to wonder if they've ever been exposed to any. Maybe what they really hate is the joyless, boring rigor of memorizing

---

[1] However, everything imaginable has been tried in a desperate search for one. The leading candidate, as of this time, is blind dumb luck.

[2] If the people around you *are* guidance counselors, you may include them or skip this exercise altogether. This is a judgement call.

"fundamentals."[1] This is particularly likely if the purpose for knowing this information has never even been mentioned.

Maybe if they were exposed to the intriguing *ideas* of physics and biology they would find they don't hate them so much after all. Sure, if they want a career in science they will sooner or later need to have those fundamentals firmly etched in their memories, but *who says* that everybody has to master them before you can move along to the good stuff?[2] Adults don't have to do that. They can learn anything they want to in any order they please.

---

[1] Teachers may worry that the instructors who get their students in the next grade or at the university will fault them for not teaching the fundamentals. Don't worry about that. They do that *now!* How could it possibly be any worse if you teach some really interesting science?

[2] Please note that it is a fact that no examination or academic prerequisites are required to purchase a subscription to Scientific American or any other science magazine.

The Mall of Science

*T*he sciences can be categorized in any number of ways. The divisions are somewhat arbitrary and there is much overlapping. There are so many sub-disciplines that it would be next to impossible to list them all. In school though, they are usually broken out as shown below. Your own peculiar scientific interest fits in here somewhere.

The Sciences

Biology – Animals and plants
Botany – Plants
Zoology - Animals
Ecology – Biological interrelationships

Chemistry – Atoms and molecules
Biochemistry – Atoms and molecules of life
Inorganic chemistry – The rest of the atoms and molecules

Physics – Mass-energy, space-time, waves and particles
Astronomy – Stars, planets, galaxies
Thermodynamics - Energy
Nuclear physics – Atoms and particles
Earth Science – Well, duh.

There are many ways to look at science. Here is another:

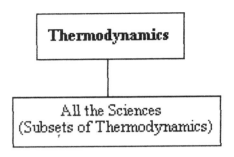

Practitioners of each of the branches can explain at length why their field is the most critical to human existence and why it is not particularly important to know anything at all about the other branches. The brighter ones of course don't do this and that provides an excellent sorting mechanism for separating smart scientists from stupid ones. You rarely have to wait very long for those in the latter category to sort themselves.

Each of the branches has it own vocabulary. There are sets of buzzwords that will make you *sound* literate. Actually, when you think about it, *sounding* literate is pretty much indistinguishable from *being* literate isn't it? You might not be found out for years.

Here then is an incomplete list of words and phrases from some of the assorted branches. Looking up the words will lead to other words and to the fundamental ideas and models. The phrases are just for sub-cultural background.

Biology: DNA, cells, genes, genome, chromosomes, phylum, genus, species, specialization, adaptation, *"He's dead, Jim"*, niche, food chain, ecology, biome, sex

Chemistry: Valence, bonding, precipitate, displacement, reagent, *"Don't pour that in there!"*, glassware, isotope, ion, suspension, endothermic, *"They'll grow back."* , exothermic, gas chromatograph, lawsuit

Physics: Wave, particle, force, oscillation, *"You're just making this up aren't you?"* tension, entropy, acceleration, velocity, electromagnetic spectrum, spectral class, velocity vector, center of mass, *"Quantum effect I reckon."* inertial reference

Scientists in the various branches have developed unique subcultures through years of self-contamination. Biologists *look* like biologists. Physicists look like physicists and chemists look like pharmacists. Biologists are sloppy dressers and they wear comfortable shoes. Physicists are bald because they are all old and male, and chemists wear lab coats all the time, even at the beach.

These are stereotypes of course, and could be dismissed altogether if they were not so accurate. I am being facetious. There are young female physicists certainly, and there are at least fourteen biologists who are believed by some members of their families, to be snappy dressers. The part about the chemists though, that's true. Most of them don't own even a single shirt.

Scientists study systems and phenomena in order to understand their dynamics. They want to understand the thing works and how that thing interacts with its environment. The environment of all systems is other systems. It can get very complicated.

Some systems are simple and straightforward and others are very complex. Scientists often look for cause and effect relationships. Sometimes the cause-effect connection will cross the boundaries between disciplines. If unsupervised, they may cross all sorts of boundaries and run completely amok! In an extreme example, there is a line of inquiry in Meteorology and Geology that leaves the physical sciences altogether and wanders over into social science.

When weather patterns and seismic data are associated with demographic data, a bizarre pattern emerges. Wherever there are Baptists, there are tornadoes. Where you have large Catholic populations you will find hurricanes and where Buddhists settle, there will invariably be earthquakes and volcanoes. This is absolutely real! Check it out for yourself.

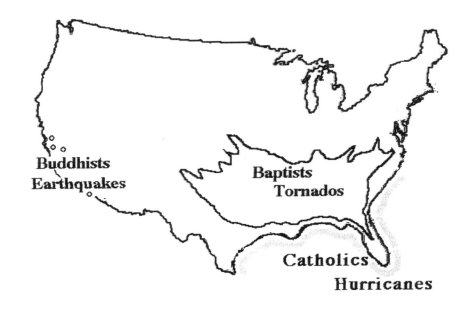

Which is the cause and which is the effect? Is it possibly just coincidence? Certainly prevailing religious thought has no effect on weather, does it? On the other hand, could particular environmental conditions attract specific human behavioral types? Is there some relationship between dietary preference, regional indigenous vegetation and religious choice? Perhaps, as with race, it is simply an effect of local eddies in the gene pool.

Human racial diversity of course is a result of localized preponderance of genetic material, accounting for biologically insignificant differences. People look different. That is because they look like their parents. Their parents probably lived *near* each other at some point. Wherever that was, people around there probably looked pretty much alike. As in real estate, the three most important principles of genetics are location, location, location. If sperm were airborne we would all be about the same color.

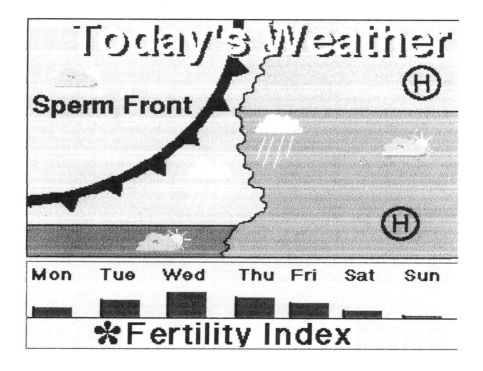

Today's Weather

Sperm Front

(H)

(H)

| Mon | Tue | Wed | Thu | Fri | Sat | Sun |

＊Fertility Index

Such issues rightfully belong to the Anthropologists and Sociologists. Even if they don't, these disciplines need the work so I am giving it to them free of charge. Besides, the Meteorologists are up to their ears in El Nino and global warming. They just don't have time for it and most of them are Lutherans anyway so, on a personal level, they are more interested in snowstorms.

It is common for legitimate research paths cross over into other disciplines. When this happens, specialists from different fields may team up. This can produce a kind of intellectual cross-pollination that is very healthy and productive. This confluence of seemingly unrelated lines of research might produce results that would never have emerged from a single narrow path.

The subdivisions of the sciences originated in the past. They were always somewhat arbitrary and they may be less sensible now than they used to be but it is difficult to change such things once established. We have addressed this problem by calling into being a long list of sub-disciplines and specialties.

One example is Polymer Science. Now here is a field built entirely around one particular category of molecules! That's pretty specific isn't it? Well, maybe no more specific than Invertebrate Marine Zoology or Solar Gamma Ray Physics or Hypersonic Fluid Dynamics. The only real limitation to increasingly fine focus is the size of department office doors. If the division's name takes longer to read than the admissions application, then you may have already made an irrevocable career decision just by spending so much time in the building.[1]

Taxonomy is the science of classifying plants and animals. It once rightfully belonged to Biology but the word has been stolen so often that Biologists have very little legitimate claim remaining. It has come to mean practically any classification system for anything. There are now taxonomies of practically everything that has discrete classifications. Taxonomies are used to break down and compartmentalize complex interrelationships.

The pseudo-science of astrology is not science but it is *full* of detail. It has as many layers of complexity as some of the legitimate sciences. It doesn't *do* anything certainly, but it *is* very complicated.

There are of course many established taxonomies of science. We certainly don't need another one. That fact unfortunately, has proven an insufficient deterrent. Herewith then, is yet another taxonomy of science. This one incorporates most of the common annoying and disturbing oversimplifications, so it may serve science professionals in the task of redefining themselves for the public at large

This one is called McMurtray's Taxonomy of the Sciences because that is what it is. It is no more useful than its predecessors but it is newer. I certainly hope it will not make me famous because it's not really the sort of thing for which I'd like to be remembered. There is however, a point to be made here.

---

[1]   In general, the number of words in your degree is inversely proportional to the number of available positions for employment in your field.

88

McMurtray's Taxonomy of the Sciences

Wet Science
    Chemistry
    Biology
    Oceanography
    Meteorology
Dry Science
    Physics
    Geology
Warm Science
    Neuroscience
    Anthropology
    Human Anatomy
Cold Science
    Astrophysics
    Nuclear Physics
    Archeology
    Paleontology

This system is as defensible and logical as any. Assuming that it matters at all where one science ends and another takes up, you can use this taxonomy to sort them all out. In any such system, the borders will be very blurry and subject to change. The logic of this classification system is self-evident but some of the finer points need elaboration.

"Warm Science" does not denote "easy" or user friendly or anything of that sort. It refers solely to the relationship or "nearness" of the objects under study to human beings. The "people sciences" are warm. "Cold Science" means removed from ordinary experience or "far away." Nuclear Physics might be strongly associated with heat in your mind but it deals with atoms and atoms are about as much smaller than a human being as a star is bigger than a human being so it's Cold Science. It is removed from ordinary sensory experience.

Meteorology is important to people so it might be a warm science if it were not so strongly tied to the transport of water. It may be warm, but not so warm as it is wet. It might even be a dry science because of all the physics in it but its intrinsic wetness overpowers that dimension.

The Wet Sciences are the ones where you mess around with liquids or things that are wet. Oil is a liquid but it does not belong to Wet Science. Petroleum is Dry Science because it is part of Geology. Sure it came from organic material and that's wet science, but that was a long time ago. Geology is strongly interrelated with all the wet sciences but the nature of the work itself is mostly dry.

Oceanographers are physicists I guess, but nothing in the physics of oceans makes much sense without Chemistry, Meteorology, Geology, Biology and Thermodynamics. Oceanographers and Meteorologists now speak of a "world ocean" meaning that planet-wide layered sphere of fluids that is liquid at the bottom and gasses at the top. Since they freely and constantly exchange mass and energy both horizontally and vertically, it makes very little sense to study the water ocean and the atmosphere separately. It's not two separate things. It's one thing.

Archeology and Paleontology are cold sciences because of their temporal separation from live humans. Anthropology is definitely warm. See how this works? Thermodynamics of course is part of everything. Generally, it refers to that part of any science that nobody really understands or likes to talk about.

Within the system described above there are hyphenated classifications as well. Medicine is a wet-warm science because it is human biology. It would be listed as a warm science because it is warmer than it is wet. The study of volcanoes (part of Geology) is cold-dry science even though there is a lot of heat and frequently a lot of water associated with volcanism.

If your particular favorite discipline is not listed, that is because it is subsumed by one of those that *is* listed. If you feel in any way disturbed or offended by it's omission, then be assured that you are fully entitled to nurse that resentment and let it fester inside you like a malignant demon forever. Resentment is one of the few pleasures available to the easily offended. Even so, you might still enjoy working out where your science would belong in the taxonomy, had it been important enough to mention. Just follow the straightforward and flawless logic delineated above.

The standard default system looks like this:
Astronomy
Biology
Chemistry
Ecology
...all the way to
Zoology

This is the traditional system commonly used in conjunction with the Dewey Decimal System in libraries. There is also of course the "Earth, Water, Wind and Fire Taxonomy," "The Historical-Chronological Science Classification System," "The Geopolitical-Economic Taxonomy of Science" and "The Science Pain Index" used by non-science majors in choosing electives.[1]

Wet-dry, warm-cold makes about as much sense as there is to be made out of all this. Perhaps you can frame a better system though. Come up with one that is widely accepted and you will be assured of a place in history. On the downside, I doubt there is a nickel to be made in the development of taxonomies of science and I doubt that it has any real value. Still, isn't this *just* the very sort of thing professors love to make students memorize? Your name will come up every time there is an exam!

The social sciences are problematic in any taxonomy of the sciences. Some scientists, particularly the cold ones, will sometimes refer to the social sciences as "soft science." This is code for "not really science." The principles and fundamentals of these disciplines may seem imprecise and fuzzy to the physicist or

---

[1] Physics courses all carry SPI numbers over 100.

the chemist. The social sciences are perceived as containing no mathematics more complicated than statistical analysis.

Mathematics is the foundation of the caste system among the sciences, and social science suffers from a severe deficit of higher mathematics. Social science is burdened also with an unfortunate reputation for virulent, rampaging subjectivity. Human beings are very difficult to study from the human perspective and so far anyway, impossible to study from outside it.

It is both unkind and unwise to dismiss social scientists as poor relations or inferior beings. This work is extraordinarily difficult to conduct. Experiments are fragile and delicate, variables are almost impossible to control and data is easily contaminated.

Because of their own checkered past, Astronomers and Astrophysicists are sometimes the most sympathetically disposed toward the persecuted social scientist. They will sometimes even rescue them when they are encircled and besieged by marauding packs of "hard" scientists at faculty parties.

There is a field of inquiry that webs together a rich and unlikely network of science disciplines including the social sciences. The science of proxemics is the study of how we humans manipulate the space around us to communicate.[1] It involves sociology, psychology, primate research, information theory, physics, biology, anthropology, biochemistry and probably some other things that I have omitted through ignorance.

The subtle syntax of the language of proxemics is ancient. It predates our ascension to valedictorian of the class of Earth. There are phrases in the language of proxemics that we share with other primates. Gorillas and chimps speak a different dialect of this language of space but we can recognize certain similarities.

---

[1] Anthropologist Edward T. Hall defined four zones which persons keep around themselves. The term proxemics refers to the study of the use of this spatial dimension for communication. It is now quite likely that you will imagine that you see this space around everybody you meet. Sorry.

It's fairly easy for anyone to conduct informal research in proxemics. You have done lots of it yourself.[1] Airports are among the best places on Earth to study human spatial communication.

Consider the circumstances in an airport. Practically all of the travelers are strangers to each other. The airport is usually crowded and most of these people are in a hurry. Isn't it remarkable that there are almost *never* collisions? We are pressed for time. We are moving fast, thinking about something else and we are among strangers. We barely acknowledge their existence at all. We act as if we are unaware of their presence and yet, we rarely run into each other. It is so rare in fact, that we take extraordinary notice of it when it happens.

The truth of course, is that we are keenly and alertly aware of each other. We are assessing threat, announcing intentions and claiming territory constantly, just as we did a million years ago on the veldt. Simultaneously, we are also receiving important messages related to physical conditions in the environment. The data rate of this communication is incredibly high. Of course almost all of this is well below the conscious level.

---

[1]   Although we rarely verbalize them, learning the idioms of spatial communication is part of the socialization process and it is probably essential for effective human interaction.

We send messages with our posture, with our eyes, with barely perceptible body movements and, although we try very hard to ignore or deny it, with our scent. I am not speaking of pheromones here. I mean actual, unambiguous, conscious level olfactory messages. Remove the business suits, and replace the expensive carry-on luggage with pouches of animal skin and you have a better picture of the primal dynamics of the airport biome.

As you move along the concourse, you carry with you a moving ellipse of personal space. The individual occupies a position near the front of the ellipse so it is larger in the back. Other humans generally respect this ellipse and they avoid moving into it. When they do, we *always* notice the encroachment and we generally react. When we are approached from the back we turn around. We rotate the ellipse.

The shape and extent of this region of personal space varies among human cultures. Personal ellipses in western cultures, for example, are larger in both the front and rear than those in the Middle East. In humans, there are measurable gender differences in the shape of the ellipse as well. Women usually claim more space in front and on the side and significantly less space behind.

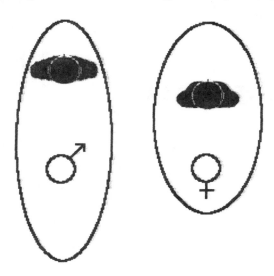

The entry of a stranger into our personal space alerts us to possible threat. There is a very short list of transactions that normally take place within this region, and not all of them are pleasant. Of course we allow friends and family members to invade our ellipse but it is forbidden territory to strangers. Even within families, respect for personal space is generally observed. One must be invited in.

We humans have developed spoken and written languages and a dazzling array of electronic communication media, but we still use the primitive territorial language that can be traced back to our pre-primate, pre-mammal reptilian ancestors. We transmit and receive this information whenever we are awake. Of course you have noticed all of this, but you may not have been aware that it is a well-established field of scientific research.

The physics of communication is fundamental to this research. We communicate through our senses. The energy flux that brings us most of our environmental data is electromagnetic radiation in the range of four to seven thousand angstroms; the bandwidth we call light. The visual channel has a data rate of 50,000,000 bits per second. That's more than 8000 times the rate of the auditory channel. In order to understand human communication it is necessary to foray into the fundamental principles of thermodynamics. Electromagnetic radiation interacts with the brain through the visual mechanisms so human physiology must be examined as well. This type of study crosses a lot of disciplinary boundaries in the sciences, and there has been some smuggling.

This field of human behavioral research incorporates the physics of light, the thermodynamics of communication, human biology, physiology, psychology, Neuro-physiology, biochemistry, primate behavior, sociology, anthropology and, as alluded to before, a bunch of other stuff. It has more than enough higher mathematics for respectability and it is just plain fascinating.

So who is doing this research? Well, it's mostly social scientists and they have had to raid the "hard" sciences in order to pursue it. While doing this they have piqued the interest of a few physicists, biologists and *"otherists"* and these folks had to go and learn a little social science in order to join the hunt.

The age of specialization lasted from September 4, 1959 to December 13, 1961. We are well past that era now, and rigid scientific specialization is no longer feasible, reasonable or intelligent. If you don't want to be a Renaissance man or a Renaissance woman, then go into something else, because you aren't going to like working in science.

One day you will be happily doing some way cool stuff in biology and then suddenly, physics will rear its ugly head. Perhaps you will be designing a high tech passenger vehicle and suddenly you will discover that you have inadvertently forgotten that people have hips and shoulders.[1] Biological science even creeps into mechanical things if people are going to use them.

If you find this distressing, then a career in science is going to make you unhappy, frustrated and mean to your dog. You won't be any good at it and you will be a pain to the people who have to work with you.[2]

Give it up then, even if your grade point average is high and the high school guidance counselor told you that you really *needed* to go into science. It's not worth the heartache you will suffer when you discover that a career in science means you are going to have to think *every damn day!* The answers will keep changing, you'll have to solve *real* problems, and you won't ever get any more A's. You will almost certainly wind up in an institution.

You want to go home now don't you? You are confused and frightened. This is not how you thought it would be, is it? Do you know where your guidance counselor lives? Maybe you could go and live there.

---

[1]   This actually happened once. It was in the aviation industry.

[2]   I have a list of names to support this statement by example but it would be unkind (and probably unwise) to include them here.

Personal Science

*T*here is a reason why we do not all learn according to the same pattern. We are different. Our brains store information in a manner that is unique to the owner/operator. All human brains we are told, contain about a hundred billion neurons.[1] We store information through complex neural interconnections. The chances that any idea or concept will be stored in separate brains with any similar pattern of neural connections, pathways and associations is so small that it can be dismissed. An idea accommodates the arrangement and neural architecture of the brain in which it resides. This is also the reason that we cannot simply depend on experts or established sources for our scientific understanding. It is necessary that we assimilate and integrate the ideas ourselves. It is we who decide what the data means.

One of the fundamental principles of Information Theory is that meaning is in the receiver.[2] That is, the receiver of a message assigns meaning to that message. It really does not matter at all what you *meant* to say. The message you *actually* sent is whatever the receiver thinks it is. The best teachers intuitively understand this. They may be happy to hear that this is validated by real science.

In any event or situation, that which is taken from the experience, that which is learned, is determined by the nature, condition and state of the individual participants. A single

---

[1]   This is the approximate count, before you have had the opportunity to kill any of them. It is not known how that number was generated or if it is reliable. It is doubtful that anybody actually counted them.

[2]   Information Theory is founded on the work of Claude Shannon and Norbert Wiener in 1949. It has profoundly impacted our lives and our economy. That it is not part of the science curriculum is inexplicable.

stimulus will have as many different responses as there are organisms responding. The residual outcome of any experience is more a matter of who showed up than what happened.

There probably *is* only *one* objective reality, but it will be understood and conceptualized differently by different observers. This is why we have reason to celebrate Einstein and Kepler, DaVinci and Gallileo, Shannon and Hummason and Pascal and the Wright brothers and Edison ...and maybe you. This is why science is *not* just the musings and models and insights of a handful of ordained scientists. It is rather the combined product of *all* our minds, working not together, but collectively. This is why it is foolish to withhold science from the unwashed and the unschooled. Not one of us is wise enough to predict who might produce some critical missing piece of the puzzle.

To really understand something you have to play with it in your *own* head for a while. The accounts and descriptions of someone else can be invaluable help, but you really have to engage the thing intellectually if you want to own it.

I will relate to you a story, which illustrates this point. This is the oldest story of our species. It actually predates the advent of written language. Indeed, it predates even the earliest records of human history. It comes to me, across the gulf of time, directly through genetic memory.[1]

Our ancestors came to self-awareness on a Thursday afternoon at 2:17 (genetic memory is obsessively precise). A long, long time ago the People awakened to full understanding of the universe and their place within it.

The world was known to be a vast flat disk arched by the dome of the sky. The People lived at the center of the disk and the Sun and stars and Moon passed over them from a point on the edge of the disk of the world to a point on the opposite side. What lay beyond the edge of the world was unknown. The edge of the

---

[1]   The existence of human genetic memory has never been established. This is just a story, okay?

world was far, far away and had never been reached even by the most adventurous hunters.

It was determined that someone must go to the edge of the world and see what lay beyond. A meeting of all the People was held to decide who should go on this trek to the edge of the world and bring back this knowledge. This meeting was called the First General Session.

The ablest and strongest of the hunters offered themselves to this great task. The council of elders considered each on his merit but it was decided that the hunters were too valuable to the tribe and could not be risked. The old Shaman explained further that none of these young men could be trusted with the powerful medicine of the knowledge of the edge of the world. That man, he said, would return to the tribe as a being of absolute power who would disrupt the institution of the ruling elders and rule the People as a tyrant.

Certainly, no member of the council could be spared for the journey. It was clear that this perilous undertaking might fail and the traveler might never return to the tribe.

One member of the inner circle proposed sending a woman. This preposterous recommendation was loudly jeered and subsequently withdrawn without a vote. The old Shaman explained the foolishness of this plan. A woman with such power would destroy the tribe, he said. If women ruled the tribe and made important decisions, the People would fall into chaos and ruin. At this point, the women, who sat on the perimeter, outside the inner circle, all laughed. We still do not know why.

After much discussion it was put forward that a small boy should make the trip. Surely a boy would pose no threat. The knowledge of the edge of the world could be brought back and shared with the ruling council in executive session. The boy traveler would share his power and be no more than a vessel for the powerful medicine of the edge.

The old Shaman rose again and struck the ground with his staff.

"Fools! he cried. A boy will forget what he has seen before the Sun can cross the sky."

He went on to say that a boy might forget to come home at all, or he might stop to explore the mouth of a crocodile.

"I will tell you how this must be done, he said. An old man shall be chosen from the tribe, one so old as to die shortly after his return. He shall carry with him a young girl, for young girls have no power and can never be a threat. Also, a small girl might prove valuable, should the need to ask directions arise. On their return the old one will die and the girl will be made a sacrifice to the spirits as soon as she has been debriefed by the council."

The solution was adopted by acclamation and was followed by the Ritual of Self-Congratulation and the ancient and sacred Celebration of Extreme Cleverness. It lasted far into the night. Great quantities of the sacred beverage were consumed.

Relatively late on the following morning an old grandfather and the youngest of his granddaughters were selected. They were supplied with the necessary protective icons and talismans and

100

other artifacts possessing powerful medicine. They were escorted to the outer boundaries of the village and there dispatched on the greatest adventure ever undertaken by human beings.

It is a long way to the end of the world. The old man and the tiny girl walked and walked and walked. After a time, when they were far from the realm of the People, they entered into strange lands inhabited by strange and wonderful animals of unusual size and shape. Some of the animals were friendly or slow in their movements and some of these were found to taste good when eaten, but others caused evil spirits to come into the belly and make the sickness.

Slowly, they learned which animals could be eaten and which should be left alone. There were other animals also, and some of these tried to taste the old man and the girl. The growly animals were warded off by the icons and the talismans and by The Ritual of the Running and Screaming and the Climbing of the Trees.

Sometimes the old man faltered and his legs grew stiff and sore and he had to lean upon the little girl for strength. At other times the little one became so tired that she could not walk and the old man carried her in his arms. The little girl took up a chant to help the old man in his walking. She sang: "Grandfather, are we there yet" and he would respond: "Almost there, just a little longer."

They came upon great mountains, which took many days to cross. They came upon great rivers and were nearly drowned in the traverse. They came upon towering trees that reached up all the way to the dome of the sky and upon great canyons, so deep that they seemed to cut right through the hard disk of the world to the very motherboard of creation.

The greatest of all the discoveries was other tribes; other "people." At first glance they seemed normal in their aspect but upon closer view, they revealed themselves to be strange beyond belief. They wore feathers as adornments instead of bones and they played strange music on different drums. Some were very frightening and all spoke with different sounds and odd gestures.

Some were tall and thin and others were short and wide. These tribes of course lived far from the center of the disk and were not "The Chosen." The old man traded with the strange ones and collected many strange treasures and articles of unknown power.

They traveled on through lands of incredible cold where snow covered everything. They crossed great barren desserts where nothing grew but sand and misery. The came upon dense forests, lush with strange plants and filled with peculiar birds. They skirted great seas that were too wide to swim. They walked, and walked, and walked. After a long, long time they came within sight of the edge of the world.

In the distance they saw the place where the great red Sun fell below the edge of the world to hide from the scary darkness until the light returned on the far side and it was safe to rise again. After a long rest and some food, they set out for the edge. On and on they walked for days and days. At night they rested. Looking back in the direction they had come, their footprints seemed to disappear into the distance. The edge of the world seemed no closer.

They spoke little. The little girl stopped her chant. Their eyes remained fixed on the far away edge as they walked. At last they arrived at the edge of the world. They fell upon the ground in despair.

Standing there, at the edge of the world was a high wall. It was taller than a man can reach, taller than a man can jump. The wall stretched away as far as they could see in both directions. The land near the wall was barren and as smooth as glass, as black as night. There were no footholds or depressions in the great wall, no place to grasp or climb. For a long time they sat in silence.

Finally the old man got up and approached the wall. He extended his arms as far up as they would stretch and then he turned and called to the little girl.

He measured her, and in his mind he added her height to the extent of his arms. It would work. Her eyes showed that she understood and she nodded. They were much too tired for the Ritual of Self-Congratulation or the Celebration of Extreme Cleverness.

The old man gathered all his strength and lifted her as high as he could reach. He held the child's thin legs at the knees. He felt her lighten as she grasped the top of the wall with her tiny fingers, and pulled, and stretched, and looked over the edge.

The old man felt her body stiffen. Her breathing stopped then started again. She trembled. Her pulse raced and then was slow. Except for her breathing she was motionless. Silent tears ran down her cheeks and fell upon the old man's head. For a long time they stood.

The old man called upon all his power to hold the child aloft. He leaned his face against the cool surface of the wall. He closed his eyes and locked his arms and fingers. When the pain became unbearable, still he held her up. When the muscles began to spasm, still he held her up. And then, she went limp. As if crumbling into his hands, she started to slip down the smooth surface. His arms buckled and they pooled together at the base of the wall.

The silence was broken only by their ragged, labored breathing. The old man looked at the girl. Her eyes shone with an odd light. Her gaze was fixed at a distance that human vision had never known. Slowly she focused on his wrinkled ancient face. She smiled a smile of purest joy and tears glazed her eyes again.

"Oh Grandfather!" she said.

"What did you see?" he said. She reached for her Grandfather and held his face in her tiny hands.

"Oh Grandfather!"

"What did you see my child?"

"Oh Grandfather!"

"Yes, I am here, but *what* did you see?"

"Oh Grandfather   "

"Yes... Tell me...What did you *see*? ...*Granddaughter, please, tell me. What did you see?*"

"Grandfather, ... You just had to *be* there."

Epilogue:

Many have been to the edge since that time, and in all the intervening centuries, no one has ever brought back the power of the knowledge of the edge of the world. The old still bring the young to the wall to hold them up to look over the edge. The old can never see it for themselves and the young must be held up by someone.

Acknowledgements

Special thanks to _____
(Your name here)

without whose invaluable assistance and support, this book could not have been written. Our many conversations on the topics covered here were extraordinarily helpful. I don't specifically remember any of them, but I guess we must have had some. If we didn't, then I'm sure you will agree that we *might* have had such conversations if circumstances had permitted. Sorry about forgetting your name, I meet lots of people and you were just one of them. Maybe you'll get mentioned in some other book.

My wife and children, friends and professional colleagues read the early drafts and made invaluable suggestions. Many inflammatory and outrageous remarks were omitted because of their wise counsel. They have also provided me with many good ideas. In addition, it should be noted that if not for the services of an excellent professional editor, my sometimes ambivalent attitude toward punctuation might have rendered much of this unreadable.

The author also wishes to acknowledge all of the authoritative sources, living and dead from which all validity flows. Maybe they weren't always right but they were always valid and I guess that's what really matters. Of course it is neither possible nor necessary to cite them all by name because, God knows who they are.

Bibliography

Now what on Earth did you expect to find back here? Did you suppose that after all that business about argument from authority being worthless, some would be cited anyway?

The contributions of scientists and others are acknowledged in the text and footnotes. Citing sources back here isn't going to guarantee the truth or respectability of any of the information or opinions in the book now is it?

The contents of this book are the opinions, flawed recollections, wholesale fabrications, and idle conjecture of the author. Maybe I made most of it up. That is for your determination. Anyway, I won't defend any of it. If you find any of the arguments compelling, then you're welcome to them. If you doubt them, then you are already well along on your journey toward scientific literacy.

The single authority for the validation of this work is the reader. Actually, that's probably the way it is with any book. Therefore, I thank you ... and the horse you rode in on.

James W. McMurtray, August, 1999

James W. McMurtray

Jim McMurtray is a six foot tall, bald headed, silver back male primate with a heavy beard and long, bushy eyebrows. He is a former planetarium director and teacher of Astronomy. He has written and produced several planetarium shows including the nationally distributed Starlight, an instructional program on the physics of stars, in 1980.

He joined the faculty of Oklahoma State University in 1981 and is now a member of the staff of the university's Department of Aviation and Space Education. In that capacity, he has been attached to NASA's Aerospace Education Services Program. He has conducted lectures, workshops, demonstrations, and seminars on the missions and programs of the National Aeronautics and Space Administration. He has presented at conferences throughout the United States and in Mexico, Puerto Rico and Venezuela. He is currently assigned to the John C. Stennis Space Center in southern Mississippi and actively involved in a variety of systemic reform efforts in education.

McMurtray has never made a career decision but accepted a series of jobs that were offered to him while he was doing something else. He has been in school since the age of six and has obtained various degrees because they were a condition of continued employment.

Just like everyone else, Jim is an expert in human communication and human behavior. He has been directly and personally involved in human behavior, both as an active participant and as a detached observer, for over fifty years. He does not always follow his own advice but he has enormous respect for it.

Jim is a member of the National Science Teachers Association, the National Council of Teachers of Mathematics, The International Technology Education Association, the National Staff Development Council, The National Council for Geography Education and the Mississippi Bowie Knife Bear Hunters Association.

Despite his qualifications, he believes that experience and credentials are a flimsy substitute for creativity, insight and intelligence. He is married and has five children and three grandchildren. He is considered a barbarian in some circles.